MICHAEL HONE

CESARE

BORGIA

His Violent Life

His Violent Times

Cesare Borgia

Cover painting: *The Destruction of Sodom and Gomorrah* by John Martin.

**Revised and Enlarged Edition
© 2018**

My books include: *Cellini* [a fully-revised 2018 edition], *Caravaggio* [a fully-revised 2018 edition], *Cesare Borgia, Renaissance Murders, TROY, Greek Homosexuality, ARGO, Alcibiades the Schoolboy, RENT BOYS, Buckingham, Homoerotic Art (in full color), Sailors and Homosexuality, The Essence of Being Gay, John (Jack) Nicholson, THE SACRED BAND, German Homosexuality, Gay Genius, SPARTA, Charles XII of Sweden, Mediterranean Homosexual Pleasure, CAPRI, Boarding School Homosexuality, American Homosexual Giants, HUSTLERS, Omnisexuality, the Death of Gay and Straight Sex* **and** *Christ has his John, I have my George: The History of British Homosexuality.* **I live in the South of France.**

Alexander VI – Monster or Saint?

DEDICATION

I dedicated my book *Caravaggio* to Cosimo and Lorenzo de' Medici, fathers of the Renaissance. For this book I'll go to the opposite end of the scale and dedicate it to absolute evil: Cesare Borgia himself, without the likes of whom the earth would be a dreary planet indeed.

CHRONOLOGY

As I prefer to tell a story completely, even if that means not following a strict timeline, I've prepared this chronology in which events are in their proper order.

1417 Alfonso V of Aragon makes Alonso Borgia his secretary.
1431 The Birth of Rodrigo Borgia, future Alexander VI.
1432 Office of the Night established in Florence.
1442 Alfonso becomes Alfonso I of Naples (1442-1458).
1443 Giovanni Bentivoglio rules Bologna (1443-1508).
1456 Rodrigo Borgia is made a cardinal.
1457 Rodrigo Borgia is made vice-chancellor.
1458 Ferrante (Ferdinand I) of Naples (1458-1494).
1460 Rodrigo told by Pius II to stop his orgies.

1466 Galeazzo Maria Sforza Duke of Milan (1466-1476) commissions da Vinci's *The Last Supper*.
1471 Francesco della Rovere elected Pope Sixtus IV.
 Six of his nephews-cum-lovers-cum-sons named cardinals.
 Ercole d'Este I – Duke of Ferrara (1471-1505).
1475 Birth of Cesare.
1475 Birth of Juan Borgia.
1478 The Pazzi and Girolamo Riario try to kill Lorenzo *Il Magnifico*..
1489 Ludovico Sforza Duke of Milan (1489-1500).
1480 Birth of Lucrezia Borgia.
1492 Death of Lorenzo *Il Magnifico* de' Medici.
 Rodrigo Borgia becomes Alexander VI.
1493 Lucrezia maries Giovanni Sforza/Jofrè marries Sancia of Aragon.
 Alexander divides the world between the Spanish and the Portuguese.
1494 Death of Ferrante of Naples; son Alfonso II takes his place.
 Charles VIII invades Italy in hopes of taking Naples.
 The beginning of the Renaissance Wars.
1495 Alfonso II abdicates in favor of his son Ferdinand II.
 Charles VIII meets Alexander in Rome.
1496 Frederick King of Naples (1496-1501).
1497 Juan Borgia murdered, certainly by Cesare.
 Lucrezia divorces Giovanni Sforza.
1498 Lucrezia's lover Pedro Calderon murdered by Cesare.
 Charles VIII hits his head against a doorframe and dies.
 Lucrezia marries Alfonso of Aragon, Sancia's brother.
 Savonarola burned at the stake.
1500 Cesare takes Forlì and Imola and captures Caterina Riario Sforza, later imprisoned in Sant'Angelo.
 Lucrezia's beloved Alfonso strangled under orders from Cesare.
 Louis XII invades and takes Milan.
1501 Lucrezia married Alfonso d'Este, both unfaithful.
 Louis XII takes Naples (as King Louis III 1501-1504).
1502 Death of Astorre Manfredi, killed by Cesare after an orgy.
 Machiavelli meets Cesare, the foundation for his *Prince*.

1503 Revolt against Cesare and death of Vitelli, several Orsini and others.
The Spaniard Gonsalvo captures Naples for Spain.
Alexander VI dies/Cesare deathly ill.
Pius III elected and is immediately followed by Julius II.
1504 Cesare goes to Spain and is imprisoned.
Isabella of Spain dies.
Michelangelo's *David* finished.
1505 Alfonso I d'Este Duke of Ferrara (1505-1534) - husband of Lucrezia Borgia.
1506 Cesare escapes prison and flees to Navarre.
1507 Cesare dies in battle.
1509 Caterina Riario Sforza de' Medici dies in a convent.
1514 Leonardo finishes his chef-d'oeuvre *John the Baptist*.
1519 Da Vinci dies. Lucrezia dies in childbirth.

Thought to be Lucrezia by Bartolomeo Veneto

CONTENTS

INTRODUCTION
Page 10

PART I
CESARE BORGIA
HIS VIOLENT TIMES

CHAPTER ONE

COSIMO DE' MEDICI
THE BIRTH OF THE RENAISSANCE
Lorenzo de' Medici, Piero de' Medici, Florence, Duke Filippo Maria Visconti, Gian Maria Visconti, Francesco Sforza, Galeazzo Maria Sforza, Federico da Montefeltro, Bartolommeo Colleoni, Filippo Lippi, Ghiberti, Brunelleschi, Dracula, Botticelli and the Borgia children
Page 16

CHAPTER TWO

THE PLOT TO MURDER LORENZO *IL MAGNIFICO*
Lorenzo de' Medici, Galeazzo Maria Sforza, Caterina Sforza, Sixtus IV, Girolamo Olgiati, Lampugnano, Carlo Visconti, Federico da Montefeltro, Girolamo Riario, Francesco Salviati, Francesco de' Pazzi, Bernardo Baroncelli, Giuliano de' Medici, Jacopo de' Pazzi, Ferrante King of Naples, Savonarola
Page 32

CHAPTER THREE

THE ORIGIN OF THE BORGIA PAPACY
Alonso Borgia (Alfons de Borja) the future Calixtus III, Alfonso V of Aragon, Queen Joanna of Naples, Ferrante I, Cardinal d'Estouteville, Cardinal Piccolomini, Pius II, Paul II,

Vannozza de' Catanei, Innocent VIII, Alexander VI, Cesare Borgia, Lucrezia Borgia, Juan Borgia, Paul III, the Great Schism, Skanderbeg, Pierluigi Borgia
Page 38

CHAPTER FOUR

THE INVASION OF CHARLES VIII
Ludovico Sforza, Gian Galeazzo Sforza, Savonarola, Piero de' Medici, Cardinal della Rovere, Alexander VI, Giovanni Sforza, Cesare, Alfonso II of Aragon, Frederick IV of Naples, Jofrè Borgia, Sancia, Louis XII, Ferrante, Charles VIII
Page 51

CHAPTER FIVE

THE DEATH OF JUAN BORGIA
Cesare, Jofrè Borgia, Giovanni Sforza, Louis XII, Frederick of Naples, Alfonso of Naples, Pedro Calderon
Page 60

CHAPTER SIX

LOUIS XII
Cesare's syphilis, his marriage to Carlotta of Navarre, the murder of Alfonso, Pietro Torrigiano, the Romagna, the Malatesta
Page 66

CHAPTER SEVEN

CATERINA SFORZA
Galeazzo Maria Sforza, Girolamo Riario, Sixtus IV, Astorre Manfredi, Antonio Ordelaffi, Ravaldino, Bishop Savelli, Ottaviano Riario, Galeotto Manfredi, Lorenzo *Il Magnifico*, Innocent VIII, Erasmus, the Gutenberg Press, Alfonso d'Este, Alexander VI, Giacomo Feo, Giovanni de' Medici
Page 74

CHAPTER EIGHT

ASTORRE MANFREDI MURDERED IN ROME
CATERINA SFORZA DIES IN FLORENCE
Faenza, Francesca Bentivoglio, Gianevangelista Manfredi, Caterina Riario Sforza de' Medici, Giovanni de' Medici, Giovanni dalle Bande Nere, Siena, Bernard Stewart d'Aubigny, Machiavelli
Page 92

CHAPTER NINE

THE REVOLT OF THE CONDOTTIERI
Vitellozzo Vitelli, Paolo Vitelli, Oliverotto of Fermo, Magione Orsini, Paolo Orsini, Roberto Orsini, Francesco Gaimbattista Orsini, Ermes Bentivoglio, Pandolfo Petrucci, Alexander VI, Ramiro de Lorca, Micheletto de Corella
Page 102

CHAPTER TEN

THE RENAISSANCE WARS
Alexander VI, Julius II, Emperor Maximilian I, Ferdinand of Spain, Louis XII, Henry VIII, François I, Emperor Charles V, Alessandro de' Medici, Clement VII
Page 108

CHAPTER ELEVEN

THE STAGE GOES SILENT
Alexander VI, Cesare Borgia, Lucrezia Gianbattista Ferrari, Giovanni Michiel, the family d'Este, Micheletto, Pius III, Julius II, Queen Isabella of Spain, Juan of Navarre
Page 119

PART II
CESARE BORGIA

HIS VIOLENT TIMES

CHAPTER TWELVE

PERKIN
Perkin Warbeck, Simnel, Margaret of Burgundy, Richard III, Edward IV, Henry VII, Maximilian I, Philip I, War of the Roses, James IV, Ferdinand and Isabella, Charles VIII
Page 126

CHAPTER THIRTEEN

BANQUET OF THE CHESTNUTS
The Borgia, Johann Burchard
Page 141

CHAPTER FOURTEEN

LEONARDO DA VINCI
Salaì, Giovanni Melzi, Orazio Melzi, Giorgio Vasari, *The Vitruvian Man*, Giacomo Andrea, Cosimo de' Medici, François I
Page 142

POSTSCRIPT
Page 153

SOURCES
Page 154

INDEX
Page 157

INTRODUCTION

As I wrote in the Introduction to my book *Caravaggio*, Caravaggio was for all practical purposes the inventor of chiaroscuro, the extensive use of light and dark. The *scuro*--the dark part of his life--was in abundance in Caravaggio's career: violence, street brawls and at least one killing. Based on the paintings of his two principal lovers, Cecco and Minniti, both of whom developed into accomplished artists, we see what was perhaps the *chiaro* side--the light segment: languorous looks of youths in love with the man behind the brushes. The chiaroscuro as portrayed in my book on *Cellini* balances out, in that we known of his love for numerous friends, expressed without reserve in his autobiography; but the *scuro* was also present, in a number of murders, perhaps five, and in sadism towards women that one would treat as ridiculous allegations if the physical cruelty were not detailed by Cellini himself in his own writings (5).

For Cesare there is no known *chiaro*. If he cared for any living thing, even a dog, we are unaware of it. That he had Caligulan incestuous relations with his sister is attested to by several sources. That he killed his own brother Juan was witnessed by a man present when Cesare had the lad's body thrown into the Tiber ("Giving the orders in Spanish, Sire, was a man on a white charger, dressed all in black, the horse's hooves and his spurs were of silver"). He spoke filthy barnyard vernacular Italian, but was nonetheless called charming by most who knew him. He raped anything that caught his eye, including the Countess Caterina Riario Sforza de' Medici about whom much will be said later, after winning her in battle ("Well, at least she won't be wanting for fucking", said a French captain as Cesare led her away). It was during an orgy that he murdered the seventeen-year-old Astorre Manfredi, said to have been the most beautiful boy in Italy, after using his buttocks and those of Astorre's fifteen-year-old brother. He assassinated several of his sister Lucrezia's husbands, one of whom she dearly loved, when her pussy was needed to seal diplomatic alliances with ever-more important nobiliary.

Never the fool, Cesare meticulously planned for the coming death of his father, Pope Alexander VI, amassing wealth and arms. What led to his undoing made an ending not even a Hollywood production could have envisioned.

One is attracted to Cesare as one is universally drawn to malevolence, to a black hole, to the abyss. He was evil personified, this man of great height and great beauty, an accomplished athlete who amused himself with wrestling husky village lads. A warrior who knew from birth that his calling was military conquest, a destiny he acceded to over the body of the brother he slew.

The Borgia were all war and sex, from the father, Pope Alexander, the original warrior pope (even if he was supplanted by one more valiant still, Julius II, Cesare's later nemesis), whose dream was to recuperate the Papal States as a first step to reuniting all of Italy under his son Cesare, nearly 400 years before Garibaldi (4). Alexander is said to have encouraged relations between his son Cesare and Cesare's sister Lucrezia as a way of binding both to him; he's said to have inseminated son and daughter himself, as the ultimate tool of unity that nothing ever could or would tear asunder.

This book will thoroughly cover the sexuality of the period, which was essentially homosexuality for the simple reason that girls were protected with Brinks-like security, chattel to be used in furthering a family's advancement to the top of the food chain, the reason why Lucrezia Borgia was married to one boy after another. Her father Pope Alexander VI got rid of the first boy by having him declare, at the cost of his life if he refused, that he had never touched Lucrezia due to his impotence, although to friends he had bragged at having had her "a thousand times". The father of one of Lucrezia's children was cut to ribbons while literally grasping the robes of the pope, splattering the Holy Father's face with blood, while still another boy she loved was throttled on orders from her brother Cesare. As girls were thusly protected, boys, needing release, turned to other boys. But even beyond the protection of girls as an excuse for male-male relations,

Florentines cold-shouldered marriage. Only half tied the knot because the other half wished to enjoy the freedoms offered by the Renaissance, after centuries of the stifling Middle Ages. That said, those who did marry were little hampered by their wives, wives for whom marriage in itself sufficed, having been instructed by their mothers early on that their husbands would seek pleasure outside the marriage bed. The pope had so warned his daughter Lucrezia, so when he was told that her latest husband had spent the day after his marriage to Lucrezia in the company of other women, Alexander replied that this was not surprising, as the boy was young and in good health. Even in the upper classes here in France today, French women are educated to accept the inevitable, as one of my students, the very old wife of an ambassador, admitted to me, letting me know, at the same time, that she was free should the young man I was then be interested. The Italians have always had a pragmatic view of sexuality. I've been lucky in living on both extremities of France, years on the Côte d'Azur and years on the Atlantic. At the French port of Menton, a few meters from the Italian border, I was the only French boy on my quay. All the rest were rich Italians, often very old, who, without exception, *without exception,* left the port for a day of pleasure in one of the surrounding inlets with a young girl at his side. Many Italians in their 70s were accompanied by young wives and the new families they had founded, kids from one year in age upwards. Whereas on the Atlantic coast I never ever saw an elderly Frenchman (all *middle class*) sail off for a day of fishing accompanied by anyone other than his grey-haired spouse.

    The paradox is that while every male in Florence was doing it with other males, the Florentine government set up the Office of the Night whose unique purpose was the extinction of acts of sodomy. Savonarola preached against sodomy, and sodomy itself was explanation for atrocities. When Barbarossa overran the island of Lipari and massacred its inhabitants, religious souls raised their heads to the heavens and asked how God could have permitted such barbarity. The answer invariably was that it was God's will to punish the Lipariots' taste for sodomy. Often the clergy who raged against the depraved act of sodomy were--as today--the most enthusiastic practitioners, the ease of its perpetration due to the limitless number of boys who sought economic stability, during the Middle Ages and Renaissance, by becoming priests. Today the best places to go to escape homosexual opprobrium are Hollywood if one is handsome enough, the priesthood if one isn't (both places where boys are most accessible, busloads arriving daily in Hollywood, choirboys placed in the hands of those supposedly there to protect them by ignorant parents). Savonarola was burned at the stake, but his views against sodomy were shared by the masses, and even today, in our liberal society where one is now free to marry the boy of his choice, a lad would be crazy to admit, to his locker-room mates, that he preferred them to the chirping maidens in the showers next door.

All aspects of Cesare Borgia's life will be covered here, but only material germane in bringing this unique person to life. Nonessential aspects, those that must be covered in a biography presumed to encompass every facet of a person's existence, will not be recounted, which will free the space necessary to paint a far wider canvas, allowing me to fully exploit major historical events, events that made Cesare the man be became, events of such import that kings and emperors sat on the edge of their thrones awaiting news of their denouement.

The age in which Cesare Borgia lived was pitiless and lustful, an age of red and white--blood and semen. It was an age of contrasts, one in which Michelangelo wrote sonnets to his beloved Tommaso Cavalieri, while in Malta the heads of captured Turks were shot into Turk lines through cannon from the fortifications held by the monk Knights of St. John. An age where Caravaggio pushed aside passers-by while searching for trouble, where women were flattened against walls while men took their pleasure--violence that would relegate *The Clockwork Orange* to the realm of a tale for infants. It was an age of Sforza brute force and de' Medici humanism; an age of artists, painters, sculptors and architects who make our own Andy-Warholian era cower by its comparative mediocrity. An age of turbulence thankfully lacking the resources of our own enlightened times during which-- in just two major wars--we saw the end of over 60,000,000 lives.

Five hundred years have lapsed between then and now. Back then Burchard, the great historian, claimed that there were orgies organized by the Borgia who were participants; other historians, today, turn Pope Alexander into a misunderstood saint. His son Cesare is seen to be a monster by some, a dispenser of justice by others. Rafael Sabatini, in his *The Life of Cesare Borgia,* believed that most historians, then as today, diverted the truth in order to make their tale "well-salted and well-spiced." For Sabatini both Burchard and Niccolò Machiavelli are to be discounted, despite the fact that Burchard was *there.* Burchard was the Master of Ceremonies to the Vatican for 23 years, ending a year before Cesare's death. It was he who organized the sumptuous entertainment and the banquets, he who introduced the great men of the time, Charles VIII, Louis XII, among countless others, into the presence of Pope Alexander VI. It was Burchard to revealed the Banquet of the Chestnuts, during which Alexander gave out prizes for the men who could ejaculate the farthest and who copulated with the most women. Machiavelli was not only there, he rode alongside Cesare himself, and wrote an entire book on the man, *The Prince.* Many of the historians Sabatini relegated to the oubliettes--Sanazzaro, Cappello, Sanuto, Matarazzo, d'Anghiera, Guicciardini, Panvinto--had grievances against the Borgia, but on some points they all agreed with each other, which forms the basis of this work. Sabatini himself was a highly religious man who adored Alexander VI, calling him Holy Father throughout his entire book. I personally have no intention of discounting anything Sabatini put forward, as I too wasn't in wondrous Italy to witness the equally wondrous events that formed what is, for me, the most passionate period of history, the Renaissance, nor will I neglect the views of today's historians who believe that Alexander washed whiter than white. But I will nonetheless give precedence to those like Burchard and Machiavelli who were visual witnesses, as well as the others in the oubliettes who lived and wrote around the time Cesare lived.

Sodomy today refers, in one's mind, to anal sex between males. Back then it was any act other than straight-forward penile/vaginal insertion. A man going down on a woman or vice-versa was sodomy. No one was categorized as homosexual, heterosexual or bisexual because such categories were nonexistent. Most of Michelangelo and da Vinci's lovers went on to found families, something homosexuals today normally do not do (other than the British, for societal reasons, as well as film stars and politicians to protect their careers), and those who try to find marital felicity, like Nijinsky and Tchaikovsky, wind up committing or trying to commit suicide. Michelangelo and da Vinci were the exception: men who may never have "known" women. Why we put ourselves in boxes today is incomprehensible when compared to the Renaissance, when both sexes were one's oyster (6).

Whereas today sexual categories--homo, hetero, bi--are stringent, back then sexual roles were just as stringent. Men were active and boys passive; passive boys were from age 12 to age 18-- the same criteria that held forth in Ancient Greek pederasty. (Both Cellini and da Vinci are thought to have had boys from age 10, and Michael Rocke in his wonderful book *Forbidden Friendships* tells us that in Florence boys submitted passively from ages 9 to 24.) The division into active and passive, men and boys, was so evident during the Renaissance that it was never discussed, as it is in clubs today where men talk about their sexual preferences with new acquaintances before retiring to the backroom. Back then what was natural was anal sex; they did it, they didn't discuss it.

The truth that sex was permeable between the sexes can be summed up in a quote attributed to Machiavelli: "As a boy, he lured husbands away from their wives. As a man he lures wives away from their husbands," a later version of Rome's Caesar, "a man to all women, a woman to all men."

Man is stirred physically, mentally and, of course, sexually. Whether we like it or not, sex is the motor that rules the world, now as then. Cesare Borgia wanted armed power and sexual conquest, an easy equation for him as he possessed military genius and physical beauty. Another condottiere whom we'll soon meet, Federico da Montefeltro, had lost an eye in battle and compensated by having his nose surgically hollowed out so he could see in all directions with the remaining eye, but his power and wealth assured him a warming presence for his bed.

Sexual satisfaction was by far the norm in the man's world of the Renaissance, but not exclusively. Caterina Sforza, of Imola and Forlì, used her position as regent to put her stable boy into her bed, an extraordinarily handsome lad murdered by her subjects who found him wanting in class, only to be replaced by another, even more handsome, suitor. But as might made right, then as today, Caterina was conquered by Cesare Borgia who wanted her lands. He raped her before turning her over to his companions. Lucrezia Borgia was another free spirit who would have her fill of love and the loss of love, debauchery and suffering.

Our story begins with the brightest light of the period, the Florentine Cosimo de' Medici, grandfather of the future Lorenzo *Il Magnifico,* the star of the Renaissance.

PART I

CESARE BORGIA

HIS VIOLENT LIFE

CHAPTER ONE

COSIMO DE' MEDICI
THE BIRTH OF THE RENAISSANCE
Lorenzo de' Medici, Piero de' Medici, Duke Filippo Maria Visconti, Gian Maria Visconti, Francesco Sforza, Galeazzo Maria Sforza, Federico da Montefeltro, Filippo Lippi, Ghiberti, Brunelleschi, Dracula and the Borgia children

The story of Cosimo begins to the north of Florence, in the city-state of Milan, ruled by Duke Filippo Maria Visconti, a hugely ugly and hugely fat recluse who kept to his fortress away from the sight of those--ambassadors, kings, emperors and the like--who might judge his physical hideousness. He had a dream, that of becoming lord over as much of the land surrounding Milan as militarily possible, a dream that led him to attack the Romagne, home of tiny fiefdoms such as Forlì, Imola and Faenza. He also attacked the Florence of Cosimo de' Medici. He was paranoiac to the extreme, switching bedrooms as many as three times a night to avoid assassination. He murdered his older brother Gian Maria, a ruler of incredible cruelty who dressed his dogs to devour whomever he sicced them on. During one of the wars Gian Maria waged, the people of Milan, starving to death, pleaded with him to decree peace. In response he had his soldiers massacre 200, forbidding, from then on, the word ''peace'' in Milan, under pain of death. When Filippo Maria Visconti found his wife lacking in enthusiasm to be covered by his walruse-like blubber, he accused her of having an affair with a young page and had both beheaded. He then married a girl whom he expulsed from the palace when, on the wedding night, the superstitious duke heard a dog barking--an evil omen, although on another mistress he fathered an illegitimate daughter, Bianca. Before taking any decision he had his astrologers indicate the place and time for each of his actions.

Gian Maria and Filippo Maria Visconti

The attack of Duke Filippo Maria on Florence pushed Cosimo to hire a mercenary, the extraordinary Francesco Sforza. Cosimo wanted Francesco to destroy the power of Milan but Francesco Sforza hesitated before entering the city-state as he had plans to marry Bianca and take over Milan without having to wage war. His plan worked, he married the beauty, but as Duke Filippo Maria had not formally named him as his successor, Milan declared itself a republic on Duke Filippo Maria's death, a mere hiccup for Sforza who garrisoned the town and had himself declared duke. Sforza's contacts with Cosomo had been so humane and intellectually stimulating that Milan and Florence became friends. Cosimo backed Sforza financially to such an extent that Cosimo's palace became, literally, the Bank of Milan.

Venice, ever afraid of the hegemony of Milan, decided to send troops against both Florence and Milan. Florence appealed to Charles VII of France, a super power that made Venice withdraw simply by threatening to intervene. To thank Charles, Florence acknowledged France's age-old claim to Naples. Furious, Naples decided to go to war with Florence and sent troops to capture the city. Venice too decided to intervene again. Cosimo became literally sick due to the new circumstances and took to his bed. But two miracles occurred. Naples had to withdraw its army from the outskirts of Florence when France sent troops to make good on its claim to Naples, and Venice had to withdraw its troops when Constantinople fell to the Turks, the greatest threat ever to Venetian trade. For added safety, Venice united with Florence and Milan to better resist the Ottomans, and an era of peace descended over the former belligerents. To make doubly certain that peace would last, Cosimo sent the most precious of his possessions, a manuscript by Livy, to Ferrante, King of Naples-- itself now safe thanks to the timely death of Charles VII. Although a psychopath, Ferrante loved ancient learning and, overjoyed, he promised eternal peace between Naples and Florence.

So here we have the powers that will concern this story as it unfolds: Milan, Florence, France and Naples--we can't count Venice because the Serenissima was too busy making money to really care what was going on outside its lagoon waters. Rome, too, remained without papal authority, a land where livestock grazed on terrain surrounded by the crumbling marble columns of what had once been Imperial Rome, and would remain so until the advent of Alexander VI--the first and, with his son Cesare, the greatest of the Borgi, followed by Julius II, the Warrior Pope. Then all hell would break out.

    I began by referring to war and carnage. But Italy was far from the only country where we find the inhumanity of men. At the exact same moment, to the East, another despot reigned, and in line with my wish to broaden the canvas of our story, we'll now spend a very short time with Vlad the Impaler, known by his father's name, Dracul, meaning son of the dragon. His father ruled Wallachia and was a warrior who dedicated himself to the protection of Christians against the hordes of Ottomans of whom he is credited with impaling tens of thousands. As a boy Vlad spoke Romanian and learned Greek, German and Latin, combat skills as well as geography, mathematics and science. Vlad and a younger brother, Radu the Handsome, were sent by their father to the Ottomans as hostages, where they were taught warfare and horsemanship, and where Radu converted to Islam. Vlad's father was overthrown and Vlad's older brother, who should have succeeded his father, was blinded and buried alive. When Vlad eventually came to power in Wallachia he strove to increase both the defenses of the country and his own political power. He had the nobles he held responsible for his father and brother's murders impaled. When Turks arrived to reclaim tribute from Wallachia he requested that they remove their turbans in respect for his person. When they refused, he had the turbans nailed to their heads, killing them all. In revenge the Turks sent an army that Vlad defeated, the soldiers impaled with the highest stake reserved for their general. It was reported that a second Ottoman army turned back from the Danube, in horror, when they came across thousands of rotting corpses, their former comrades, all impaled. The pope and the Venetians--whose trade had been disrupted by the Turks--were wild with joy at the news. But Vlad's little brother who had converted to Islam, Radu the Handsome, came at the head of janissary battalions to destroy his Christian brother. He promised that the nobles in Wallachia, who had lost their positions and possessions because of Vlad, would recuperate their entire wealth, which led to the assassination and beheading of Vlad. Vlad's reputation for evil nonetheless spread through Germany and Russia, to our own times and theater screens. How much is true will never be known. He was said to have had children roasted and then fed to their mothers, and to have had the breasts of women cut off and forcibly fed to their husbands, before impaling them all.

Dracula
1395-1447

After the fall of Rome the lights went out over Europe. New Christians like Charlemagne were proud of their ignorance, declaring that they were above grammar. Charlemagne gave a choice to conquered peoples, either they convert or they would fall to the sword. During just one morning 4,500 were beheaded when they hesitated. In Constantinople the first emperor to convert, Constantine, watched helpless while 3,000 Christians died under the sword of other Christians over the interpretation of the new faith, and during the Fourth Crusade the city itself was sacked and the inhabitants massacred when the crusaders failed to receive the monies the new emperor promised them. Saint Augustine, after a youth of depravity, declared that a child was already polluted in the womb, as it had been conceived through lust. People converted easily thanks to the promise of an afterlife, but went on with everyday violence in which thousands died in drinking brawls, disputes and sports such as tournaments. Fear of disease and plague, invasion and famine, lightning and floods, dark forests of boars, bears and wolves, all combined to unite families in backward villages, where incest and a limited gene pool assured mental deficiency. Hunched over, afraid of every storm, medieval men lived out their existence is pure anonymity. There were no clocks, not even calendars among them, and even the century in which they lived was both unknown and of no importance. The Great Schism--a pope in Rome and another in

Avignon--was unknown to the peasants who passed their days in perpetual toil, seeking out the church at the time of baptisms, marriages and deaths, alongside priests as ignorant as they. Illiterate, pockmarked, gullible, superstitious, for them there were no changes anywhere simply because they were unaware of all. They didn't even have surnames, because none was needed. Only later, when the ancient world was rediscovered, did the individual begin to emerge from the formless masses. Then they took names in order to distinguish one from the other--the smithy became Smith, the tailor Taylor. Anonymity: nothing is known of the twenty-three generations it took to build the cathedral of Canterbury. But finally names emerged from the mist, those of da Vinci, Michelangelo, Botticelli, all thanks to the rediscovery of the ancient texts, a rediscovery and a rebirth: a Renaissance

The serpentine road from the Middle Ages through the Renaissance and on to Modern Times took centuries to unfold. It was this reemergence of the past, it was the heritage of a very distant Rome and Greece. It was the freedom of the human mind, a mind that turned to individual thought and rationalism over crass religious doctrine and its foundation--faith. Humanism is thought to be anti-religion, but at the time the humanists were believers in religion who simply wanted to reform certain religious practices. Those who no longer believed in religions, and there were certainly few, were heretics and candidates for the stake--a real-life burning bush, a strong incentive not to wander too far from the beaten track. The belief in the separation of the church and state, and the right not to believe in certain dogmas at all, would come--albeit only partially--near the 1700s, with Voltaire.

Petrarch is not only the founder of humanism, but was also the inventor of the term Middle Ages. His endeavor was to free Middle-Ages man by bringing back such thinkers as the Roman Cicero. He was aided in this by the great Boccaccio (immensely readable to this day), who also freed access to ancient works by reproducing them in the vernacular, Italian.

Cosimo de Medici & Lorenzo de Medici

In Florence, Lorenzo *Il Magnifico*'s grandfather, Cosimo de' Medici, helped found humanism along with his friend Niccolò Niccoli. A banker, Cosimo offered Niccoli the funds necessary to send him far and wide, even to the Holy Land, in search of the ancient manuscripts that would bring the words of the likes of Plato into the very living rooms and libraries of the Medici, hundreds and hundreds of volumes. Each discovery that Cosimo made, each old text he unearthed, was like Howard Carter peering into the tomb of Tutankhamen. Cosimo employed forty-five copyists to spread the liberating concepts of the ancients, assisted by Niccoli who wore a Roman toga to the embarrassment of his entourage. Greek studies became a part of Florentine university instruction and artists like Donatello and Brunelleschi built their art along classical lines. The distinction between Platonic truth and beauty and Plato's ideal republic diverged sharply with Cosimo's continued religious beliefs, among them that he was committing a mortal sin by applying, as a banker, usury to his loans. And then, each time civilization advanced a step, it seemed (and seems) that something came (comes) along to set it back, forcing men on their knees before some god or other, because of man's lack of faith in himself: wars, disease, the horrors of the Black Death, civil strife, illness, the death of a loved one, sent (sends) men back in time to the first of the species who feared fire and lightning.

Florence

The Renaissance was Florence, and Florence was the Renaissance. Why this should be so is unknown; perhaps the other great sites of the times, Naples and Milan, were too despotic, perhaps Venice too stable; Rome was out of the running because, until the intervention of Julius II, it was Hicksville, dirty and smelly, soiled by papal hangers-on and other bovines. Traditionally, Florentine merchants vied with each other in their support of the arts. Lorenzo Ghiberti was commissioned to build the doors of the Baptistery of San Giovanni, a task that took twenty years. Filippo Brunelleschi somehow capped the Cathedral of Santa Maria del Fiore with a towering roof--the enigma being how the walls of the cathedral can bear the tons of weight--that is still the city's major landmark.

Ghiberti's doors and Brunelleschi's Dome

Today we make an industry of searching each other out; huge amounts of time and energy are dedicated to the enterprise. In Italy sex between males was but a strand of the social tissue. Men worked, studied and played together; they engaged in games and sports and cultural pursuits; they associated professionally or labored side by side. And when the mood and/or occasion was right, they shared a joint orgasm, a way of relief as was playing ball or swimming or horseracing, fencing or tournaments. It was natural in the way that sex should be. It was not the concentrated effort to rack up the greatest number of sexual experiences or glee over the abundance of boys/girls one inseminated, as found in today's dormitories. The occasional release alongside the buddy who was at hand (literally) was the norm, in the same way that they ate and drank together.

It took the Dark Ages to make sodomy a crime. In ancient Rome male-male sex was simply an alternative means to pleasure. Amusingly, the exception to the prohibition of same-sex sex didn't apply to *boys* in Italy, boys who could literally do anything they wanted among themselves. For their parents, sex during adolescence was simply the discovery of one's body: what brought it pleasure, what brought it pain; what worked and what didn't; which zones were erogenous and which were not. It was discovery--to the adolescent boy far more important than

Columbus's fumbling onto the Americas. It was sexuality; it was in no way *homo*sexuality.

It was known that Cosimo's grandson, the great *Il Magnifico* himself, had a marked preference for boy buttocks. The preference was illegal but so prevalent that it was rarely prosecuted. But *rarely* prosecuted still meant that there were thousands of cases brought before the courts, which shows the prevalence of the phenomena. A man could be castrated for having sex with a boy (the ultimate cure!); boys 14 to 18 had to pay a fine of 100 lire; boys under 14 paid 50 lire (although ages 9 to 12 generally got off scot-free, following a stern sermon). Foreigners could be legally beaten by whoever caught them *in flagrante delicto*, and if found guilty by a tribunal they could be burned at the stake. In reality no one was much bothered unless he raped a young boy or had sex with children. Consensual sex was more or less admitted; it was the coercive variety that was prosecuted.

Every boy wanted to marry a virgin. So boys who tried to seduce girls could find themselves in mortal danger as families were set on protecting their capital, their virgin girls, girls who served to form the alliances so necessary during the Renaissance. A girl deflowered was no longer an asset. To the contrary, she exposed her family to the open ridicule of the nobility. On the other hand, it was accepted that boys needed physical release. The least harmful means of such release was between themselves, a measure that was silently but fully acknowledged.

Naturally, boys could pay for sex in whorehouses or on the street, especially around the old market called the Mercato Vecchio. Alleys at night often saw prostitutes lined up against walls while the boys humped them through the drop-fronts attached by ribbons that could be rapidly untied. Boys adored ornamenting themselves in skin-tight trousers, leaving nothing of their muscular buttocks to the imagination. The cloth drop-fronts were often replaced by codpieces of immense dimensions, as alluring to maidens as were the boys' gestures, their hands stroking the immense bulges, or caressing the curvature of their own asses.

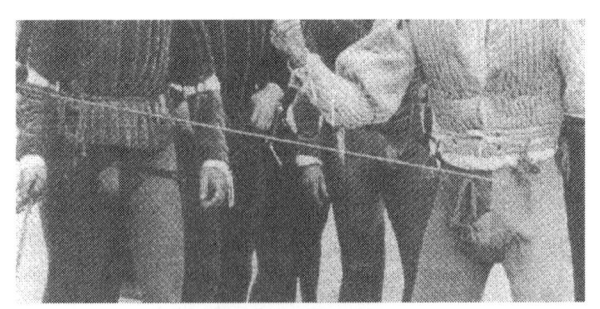

Cloth drop-fronts

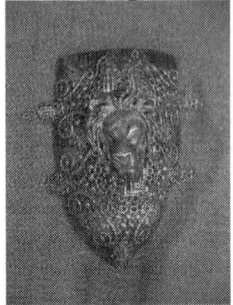

Codpieces

As a banker Cosimo needed papal business due to the prestige that affiliation with the church represented to the world. He therefore cultivated certain men whom he felt might become pope (in the same way he had cultivated the condottiere Francesco Sforza who eventually became Duke of Milan and an enormously important ally). One such man was Parentucelli, a bookworm about whom it was said that anything he did not know was beyond human understanding. Cosimo lent him vast sums of money to buy manuscripts. When Parentucelli became Pope Nicholas V, Cosimo helped him found the Vatican Library modeled after Cosimo's own. After Pope Nicholas came Pope Pius II, said to have been the Vatican's first humanist. He loved wine, women and honors, all of which Cosimo provided him when he came to Florence. Pius II tried to suppress a book he had written as a youth, *The Tale of Two Lovers*, supposedly full of erotic imagery. The suppression of the book failed and it became a Renaissance bestseller.

Another artist in Cosimo's service was Fra' Filippo Lippi. Headstrong and uncontrollable, his aunt placed him in a monastery when he was fifteen, where he later took his vows. When he discovered that he had a natural gift for drawing, he made his way to Padua to study art. A womanizer who fathered at least one known son, he went to Ancona where, out sailing, he was captured by Moors and sold into slavery in Africa. Although human portraits were forbidden by Muslims, he drew the local caliph who was so impressed that he freed him. Through the vagaries of life Lippi found himself in Florence working for Cosimo, but his taste for drink, women and bar fighting kept him from his art. In response, Cosimo had him locked in his studio where he ate, slept and painted. He escaped and was found weeks later drunk and whoring. Cosimo tried a different tactic. He sent him into the country, out of reach of enticements, where, even so, Lippi met a nun he made pregnant. Cosimo arranged things through Pius II, the pope known for his erotic literature, who allowed the nun and the artist to marry. But before the marriage took place the nun's family poisoned him, although other sources believe he was poisoned by another mistress because of his continued interest in the nun. In any case, he *was* poisoned and Cosimo's grandson Lorenzo had a monument raised to him, built by Lippi's son who had, by then, become an artist just like his dad, Filippino Lippi.

Filippo Lippi self-portrait

    Cosimo the great humanist died, but not before fathering Piero who in turn fathered the great Lorenzo *Il Magnifico* de'

Medici. The image of Cosimo that I love best is reported by an ambassador who, when he visited him, found him in bed between his two sons, Piero and Giovanni, one old man and two others middle-aged, all three suffering from gout.

His son Piero was called the Gouty, a disease that attacked the wealthy who could afford meat and rich sauces and who disdained vegetables considered peasant food or animal fodder. The result was the retention of uric acid which crystallized in the joints causing incredible pain. Piero married Lucrezia Tornabuoni, a chance for his son Lorenza, the future *Il Magnifico*, because of her forceful nature and intelligence.

Piero was no banker compared to his father Cosimo. He rarely foreclosed debts and loaned funds to the likes of Edward IV of England who battled for years with Henry VI to see which of them would finally become king, running up horrendous bills and then, following victory, Edward died too soon to repay them. Cosimo's squishy-squashy approach made enemies of every class from merchants to the nobility.

Piero attempted to shore up his relations with King Ferrante of Naples by sending Lorenza, superb from the heights of his seventeen years. Ferrante, a sociopath who had to be constantly wooed, could just as easily have killed Lorenzo or kissed him. Lorenzo did more than anticipated, charming the king out of his socks with his youthful candor, intelligence, sparkle and spunk.

In Milan Francesco Sforza died and was replaced by his son Galeazzo Maria Sforza, age twenty-two. Galeazzo had been trained in combat by his father and was therefore feared. When the Duke of Ferrara decided, along with Venice, to take advantage of Piero's weakness as a leader by invading Florentine territory, Galeazzo sent 1,500 troops to Florence's aid. The Duke of Ferrara discovered that, although the citizens of Florence were unsatisfied with Piero, they would not rise up against him, as the duke had been led to believe. So he retraced his steps and returned to Ferrara. The Doge of Venice continued on, however, forcing Piero to seek help from not only Naples and Milan, but also from a very feared condottiere, Federico da Montefeltro of Urbino, a city-state on the edge of the Romagna.

They all came together in the main square of Florence, the Piazza della Signoria, where Lorenzo rode up with 3,000 soldiers the Florentines had assembled, the very young Lorenzo splendid in his full armor. Galeazzo withdrew his forces for reasons he never explained, and so it was that Lorenzo's troops, and those of Federico da Montefeltro, clashed with a Venetian army led by Bartolommeo Colleoni. The battle ended indecisively even though both sides claimed victory.

Montefeltro.

By far the most impressive condottiere of the period was Federico da Montefeltro. He was a Renaissance man, the possessor of a truly wonderful bureau done in *trompe-l'oeil*. He's thought to have killed his stepbrother Oddantonio, made easy by the people of Urbino who were unhappy with his reign. Montefeltro inspired loyalty among his men, sharing his gains as condottiere with them, and because his fees were high, he was able to enrich Urbino. He had surgeons remove part of his nose so that he could see in all directions with the eye remaining him, the other having been lost in a tournament. He fought for Florence, for Milan, for Naples, and then against Florence before the Treaty of Lodi brought peace to the three city-states. The Treaty ended quarrels concerning the boundaries between the belligerents and confirmed the position of each duke, prince, count or doge as the head of his particular city-state. After the death of Francesco Sforza, Montefeltro assisted Francesco's son Galeazzo Maria Sforza in governing Milan.

Much has been said about Lorenzo's ugliness, a nose so flattened it deformed his voice and destroyed his sense of smell. His hair was straight, his chin jutting, his eyes intelligent and piercing, dark and gentle, and it is known that he attracted women. Piero sent his wife Lucrezia to Rome to find a wife for Lorenzo. The choice fell on Clarice Orsini, beautiful but scoffed at by Lorenzo's friends who found her lacking in intelligence. The match was a step up for Lorenzo because the Orsini were nobles well entrenched in the church, many of whom had been cardinals and there had even been one Orsini pope.

Lorenzo *Il Magnifico* de' Medici
1449-1492

Piero, too ill to do so himself, had Lorenzo organize a tournament in celebration of his betrothal, a contest between combatants on horses, armed with lances, aimed at unseating each other. It was said to have cost 8,000 florins while Clarice's dowry had been a modest 2,000 in comparison. There were banners and pennants and Lorenzo wore a cloak of white silk lined with scarlet. He rode a white charger given him by Ferrante King of Naples which made--given the back-stabbing tendencies of Italian politics--Galeazzo Maria Sforza of Milan green with envy. The wedding banquet lasted three days, with minstrels, tables laden with roast pig and 300 barrels of the best wine. Although Clarice and Lorenzo may never have been intellectually attuned, they were physically, as she gave him ten children. There is little doubt that more went on in Lorenzo's palaces and stables than girl-boy activities, and it is a fact that the laws against male-male encounters were relaxed to the point of near nonexistence while Lorenzo controlled Florence. The artists surrounding him--Donatello, da Vinci, Michelangelo--as well as teachers like the Greek and Latin scholar Poliziano, were homosexuals, as were a number of Lorenzo's closest companions.

Italy throughout the ages, as much today as then, is known for its *jeunesse dorée*. Lorenzo had the best education possible, thanks to his grandfather Cosimo who allowed him to participate in the meetings of the Platonic Academy he founded. His mother was versed in the arts and Lorenzo spent his life collecting the finest manuscripts, paintings, sculptures, coins and jewels--although far less of his life doing so than Cosimo. He loved riding and hunting with falcons, giving full voice to dirty songs that amused his comrades as much as himself. He was not drawn to banking but he had the gift of appointing the right man to do the job in his place. He could be a brilliant conversationalist, an ardent churchgoer, and still slum the nights away in taverns and bordellos, ending the evening in the early hours by serenading the virgin sweetheart of one of his friends--after they had all fulfilled the lustful yearnings of their young flesh. He wrote poems, one of which warned of the ephemeral nature of youth, exhorting himself to make the most of what he had--and he had plenty. Again, then as today: Italians have always been among the most sensual people on earth, and who could represent the beauty of the era better than the painter Botticelli whose *Primavera* is among the most gorgeous works of the human hand.

Botticelli's *Primavera*.
At that time in Florence there existed special letterboxes that citizens used to denounce other citizens. It was in this way that Botticelli, 1445-1510, came to the attention of the authorities. He was accused of "keeping a boy." An investigation took place but as he was well known and visibly had only a few more years to live (six, as it would turn out), the Office of the Night responsible for such cases turned a blind eye. His reputation didn't seem to have suffered as afterwards he was appointed to decide where Michelangelo's *David* would be placed in Florence.

As for Lorenzo, he was a golden boy, yes, but one who was soon to know adversities that would have brought a lesser man to his knees.

CHAPTER TWO

THE PLOT TO MURDER LORENZO *IL MAGNIFICO*
Lorenzo de' Medici, Galeazzo Maria Sforza, Caterina Sforza, Sixtus IV, Girolamo Olgiati, Lampugnano, Carlo Visconti, Federico da Montefeltro, Girolamo Riario, Jacopo Salviati, Francesco de' Pazzi, Bernardo Baroncelli, Giuliano de' Medici, Jacopo de' Pazzi, Ferrante King of Naples, Savonarola

At the death of Piero, Lorenzo was asked by the city nobility to take his place, which he did at age twenty, bowing modestly before the aged men standing before him. His first guest to his palace was Galeazzo Maria Sforza, accompanied by his soon-to-be-famous daughter, Caterina. Unknown to the nobles who requested his leadership, Lorenzo, fearing that he would be brushed aside as being too young and inexperienced, had sent messages to Galeazzo requesting troops, should he be forced to take power through arms. Galeazzo answered by putting a thousand men on the road to Florence. To thank him, Lorenzo put at Galeazzo's disposal every culinary, artistic and erotic pleasure at his disposal. Galeazzo returned to Milan decided to rebuild the city and stock it with art along the lines of Florence. Italy being Italy, Ferrante, King of Naples, became jealous of Lorenzo's influence over Galeazzo. As for Caterina, this was her first visit to Florence, the city in which she would turn to Christ when too old to receive lovers, the city in which she would die.

Lorenzo met with the new pope, Sixtus IV, and is said to have impressed the old man by his youthful vigor, although not enough so that Sixtus would give Lorenzo's brother Giuliano a cardinal's hat (Sixtus did, however, give six hats to his six nephews). Sixtus compensated by giving Lorenzo a splendid head of Augustus to the fury of Galeazzo he wanted it. Galeazzo was becoming less sane each day and, luckily for all, he was soon assassinated.

Galeazzo Maria Sforza.

Galeazzo Maria Sforza, Duke of Milan, was thought to be a psychopath who didn't hesitate to tear off a man's limbs with his own hands or rape a woman, noble or not. His sexual appetite was hard to appease but once his lust fulfilled, the woman was handed to his entourage for their needs. He detested poachers, strangling one to death on a rabbit pushed down his throat and another was nailed inside a coffin and then buried alive. A priest who predicted Galeazzo would have a short life was starved to death. Galeazzo was finally brought down by three conspirators, one of whom was a very young man named Girolamo Olgiati who, thanks to Galeazzo's library to which the duke gave him access, was able to read the lives of Brutus and Cassius and how they tried to bring republicanism back to Rome through the assassination of Caesar, a perfect example of how the ancient texts formed the Renaissance mind, Olgiati's ideal for Milan. A second conspirator, known only as Lampugnano, had obscure motives concerning land deals. The third conspirator was Carlo Visconti whose sister had been dishonored by the duke, a motive of importance today but at the time everyone was throwing his daughter or wife at Galeazzo in hopes of gaining profit. They met in church. Who struck first is in question, but the version I prefer has Visconti (the boy whose sister had been raped) on his knees as if requesting a favor as the duke walked down the nave. When Galeazzo paused to listen to him, Visconti plunged his dagger into the duke's genitals. The other men followed suit. Galeazzo, at age 32, was dead before he hit the marble flooring. The three assassins, certain of public support, did not bother to hide. Instead of thanking them, the citizens of Milan killed Lampugnano instantly and then dragged his body through the streets; the other two were caught later by Galeazzo's guard and they were disemboweled, quartered and decapitated. As he was dying one of the three is reported to have shouted out, "Death is perhaps terrible, but honor and glory are eternal!" Which may be true as I'm retelling the story *500 years* after the event.

Young Lorenzo's first military sortie was against nearby Volterra that was in Florence's sphere of influence, the cause of which was a dispute over trade dues owed Florence. Lorenzo chose the famous Federico da Montefeltro to take the city, which he did, losing, alas, control over his soldiers who sacked, raped and killed hundreds. Lorenzo went to the town to offer his excuses and make amends by handing out money. Lorenzo knew it was a situation that his grandfather and father would have defused before an eventual massacre.

Sixtus IV, who had found Lorenzo to be a darling boy, asked him, as head of the Medici banking system, for a loan of 40,000 florins in order to buy Imola. Sixtus wanted Imola as a gift to his son Girolamo Riario, whom the pope passed off as one of his numerous nephews. Because the pope already owed 10,000 florins to the Medici bank, Lorenzo hesitated, a hesitation that would cost him plenty. The pope, apoplectic, turned to the Pazzi, bankers who immediately agreed. The Pazzi were an old family with money that went way back. The manager of the Rome branch of the Pazzi bank, Francesco de' Pazzi, hated Lorenzo whom he found arrogant and far too rich for a parvenu. He hatched a plan to assassinate both Lorenzo and his brother Giuliano. For this he turned to Girolamo Riario, now lord of Imola, and Jacopo Salviati, an enemy of the Medici, whom Lorenzo had forbidden to cross Florentine territory due to Salviati's attempts to undermine Medici power. Salviati wanted to get to Pisa where Sixtus had named him archbishop and Lorenzo's refusal to let him pass deprived him of huge sums of money. The conspirators went to get Sixtus's permission "to take care of Lorenzo" which the pope gave, although piously adding that he wanted no bloodshed. The conspirators then went to see Jacopo de' Pazzi, the head of the clan, who refused his consent until he was told that the pope himself had blessed the endeavor.

On the day of the planned murders, Easter Sunday, Francesco de' Pazzi went to the Medici palace in search of Giuliano who said he wouldn't be going to church because he felt ill. Giuliano was an exception among the Medici for several reasons. Although older than Lorenzo, he was never offered a position of real power by his brother. He was far handsomer than the younger Lorenzo and liked to think of himself as a lady killer, whom his entourage mocked because he lacked his brother's charm, meaning that his bed was often empty whereas Lorenzo's never lacked for company. In addition, the youths laughed behind his back because when he did find someone, far from being the heartless enslaver of women's hearts he said he was, he would fall head over heels in love, love that invariably ended with *his* heart broken.

Francesco de' Pazzi was accompanied to Lorenzo's palace to fetch Giuliano by Bernardo Baroncelli, a banker and friend of both Francesco and the Medici. The men persuaded Giuliano to accompany them to church, giving him a friendly hug when he consented--in order to find out if he were wearing armor under his cloak.

In the cathedral Giuliano was separated from Lorenzo by a few yards. Sometime during the High Mass, thanks to a pre-planned signal, Baroncelli struck Giuliano with his dagger that pierced his brain. Francesco followed with more blows, twenty altogether, instantly killing Giuliano. Nearby two priests attached Lorenzo, one of whom nicked his neck with a dagger, but Lorenzo whipped off his cloak and held it up as protection, his sword already in his hand. As friends came to Lorenzo's aid, the attackers fled. One friend risked his life by sucking the blood oozing from Lorenzo's wound, afraid the dagger had been poisoned. Lorenzo ran to his palace, perhaps believing that his brother, whom he had not seen fall, had already returned there.

The second act of the drama took place at the Palazzo della Signoria, the Florentine Town Hall, a wonderful crenellated tower that overlooks the Piazza della Signoria which would soon possess the God-inspired statue of Michelangelo's *David*. Here Salviati, the man Lorenzo had forbidden to cross Florentine land so he could take up his position as archbishop of Pisa, led a pack of thirty mercenaries. Due to the archbishop's renown, he was allowed to enter the Palazzo della Signoria, but due to his nervousness the guards felt that something was terribly amiss. The archbishop was separated from his men who were invited into a nearby chamber that one the guards immediately locked. Government officials sounded the alarm, bells that tolled in emergencies, the ringing of which automatically set in motion the ringing of other bells in other churches surrounding Florence, until the entire countryside had been alerted and, in response, sent armed men to the Piazza della Signoria. The moment the guards at the Palazzo discovered the attempt on Lorenzo's life, they killed the thirty followers of Salviati, throwing them from the windows of the crenellated tower. Francesco was found at his palace, badly wounded by a knife blow he had inflicted on himself while stabbing Giuliano. He was taken naked to the Palazzo and hung by the neck from an upper window. Archbishop Salviati himself was flung from the same window, in full vestments. Eerily, he sank his teeth into Francesco, perhaps in revenge for getting him into such a mess, perhaps to ease the noose around his neck, perhaps due to an involuntary convulsion.

Fifty-seven-year-old Jacopo ran for his life into the country where he was recognized by peasants, arrested, sent to a dungeon and tortured. He was then taken to the Palazzo della Signoria from whose tower he too was flung, dressed only in his drawers.

His body was cut down and pulled through the streets of Florence by boys beating it with sticks before being nailed to the door of his palace, against which they banged his head, yelling out, "Open up, the master is back!" Other deaths followed, more than a hundred in all, as plotters and suspected plotters were hounded down.

Sixtus, sick with rage that an archbishop had been hung by the neck in his ceremonial robes, excommunicated all of Florence when the citizens refused to turn over Lorenzo to a papal court. The pope declared war on the city-state and turned to Lorenzo's dear friend, King Ferrante of Naples, for troops, which the king provided. The pope named Montefeltro, Duke of Urbino, to head the forces. Now old, the duke proved far less valorous than in times gone by. In the meantime, excommunication had put Florence in the position of a leper, cold-shouldered by its neighbors. Bands of armed youths descended on the city, robbing and raping and depriving it of food. Last rites couldn't be given and the dead couldn't be buried. Lorenzo, seeing that something extraordinary had to be done, took a ship from Pisa to Naples to appeal directly to his former friend Ferrante, a courageous move as Ferrante was as liable to cut off his head as to kiss him on the mouth.

Before leaving Florence Lorenzo mortgaged his castles and palaces to raise money, money he now spent like water on making gifts to the Neapolitans, on lavish festivals and on charities. It's said, though, that although he laughed at the side of Ferrante during the day, he was in despair at night. Certainly Ferrante had him visit his famous museum where he placed the dried cadavers of his enemies, pickled in herbs and dressed in what they wore when alive. When Ferrante suspected someone of plotting against him, he took him to visit his museum as a deterrent. Prior to their deaths Ferrante locked his prisoners in cages and let them go insane before starving them to death. He reigned for 36 years, and despite being a merciless and treacherous sadist, he died at age 71, perhaps receiving his just deserts in Hell. The cause of death, according to an autopsy in 2006, was colorectal cancer; he had also suffered from a double infestation of two different species of lice, in his head and in his pubic hair.

King Ferrante

Finally Ferrante, faced again with French desires to take Naples on the one hand and, on the other hand, confronted with Turkish ships that were approaching--as well as being in need of Medici banking--freed the young man. Also thanks to the Turks, Sixtus decided that he needed Florence at his side in his attempt to mount a crusade against them. He lifted the excommunication.

Lorenzo allowed the dissident monk, Savonarola, to preach in Florence where he predicted, in mid-1491, the imminent death of Ferrante of Naples and Lorenzo himself. Lorenzo died in 1492 and Ferrante in 1494.

CHAPTER THREE

THE ORIGIN OF THE BORGIA PAPACY
Alonso Borgia (Alfons de Borja) the future Calixtus III, Alfonso V of Aragon, queen Joanna of Naples, Ferrante I, Cardinal d'Estouteville, Cardinal Piccolomini, Pius II, Paul II, Sixtus IV, Giuliano della Rovere, Galeazzo Maria Sforza, Papal States, Vannozza de' Catanei, Innocent VIII, Alexander VI, Cesare Borgia, Lucrezia Borgia, Juan Borgia, Paul III, the Great Schism, Skanderbeg, Pierluigi Borgia

Pope Alexander VI was a Borgia, whose ancestors were Spanish condottieri, the warrior segment of both Alexander and his son Cesare's blood, condottieri who had chased Muslims from Valencia, taking over a good part of the lands for themselves. The most important of the first Borgia was Alonso, Alexander's uncle.

Alonso entered the university at age fourteen, leaving with two doctorates in law, one canon. Due to his expertise, he was chosen to be a member of a council set up to bring an end to the Great Schism which had seen the selection of two popes, one in Rome and one in Avignon. Rome had two families of great and competing importance, the Orsini and the Colonna, and it was a Colonna who became Pope Martin V, although there had been a hold-out, an insignificant Spaniard who was proclaimed, by the vote of three cardinals, Clement VIII. Alfonso V of Aragon was the only person to recognize him.

In 1417 King Alfonso V of Aragon, a kingdom that had absorbed Alonso's birthplace of Valencia, invited Alonso to meet with him. Alfonso was just 21 and King of Sicily, Corsica and Sardinia as well as Aragon. His sights were now set on conquering Naples ever since Queen Joanna, of disputed sanity, invited him to protect the city that was under the threat of French siege. As an enticement she decreed that he would succeed her. In point of fact, Joanna was a crazy nymphomaniac who offered her kingdom to most any male willing to "honor" her.

At the time, Naples was an immense kingdom that included the whole of the south of Italy. It was a world power that would bring Alfonso wealth, and be the first building block in Alfonso's domination over the entire peninsula, from Milan to Calabria. Naples was by far the largest city in Europe, with over 100,000 people, compared to Rome's 35,000, and its origin went all the way back to the Greeks--Neopolis. Some Neapolitans felt they were lucky to have been chosen as the capital of the empire Alfonso envisioned, although most had seen so many dukes, lords, kings, tyrants and other invaders over the centuries that they were indifferent now.

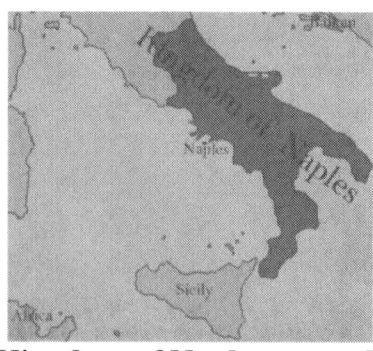

The Kingdom of Naples around 1500

Alfonso had heard of Alonso Borgia and liked him enough during their first interview to make him his secretary, with the assignment of getting Martin V's accord to his intervention in Naples. As Naples was considered to be under the jurisdiction of the church, as were the Papal States, the pope's assent was vital. Alfonso believed that Martin, tired of the feuds engendered by the Great Schism, feuds during which Spain had played a key role, would welcome him with open arms. In addition, Martin, a Colonna, was having problems as usual with the Orsini, and Alfonso felt Martin would be happy to have the virile Alfonso's backing.

The opposite occurred. Convinced by the power of France, the mightiest army then in existence, Martin threw his support behind them. Two years of war followed, during which the French killed Alfonso's brother Pedro in battle and blew his body through a cannon into the Aragon lines. In retaliation Alfonso went to Marseille and burned the city to the ground. Tired of all the fuss, Joanna, no longer convinced of Alfonso's invincibility, went over to her former enemies and declared France her legal heir.

Alfonso and Alonso Borgia, both highly intelligent, realized that the only solution to the problem would be through very fine negotiations. Alonso was assigned to contact Martin and together they worked out a compromise: King Alfonso would drop the Spanish Clement VIII and accept Martin as the one and only legitimate pope, and Martin would recognize King Alfonso's right to Naples. In thanks for his good offices, Alonso Borgia was given the bishopric of his native Valencia, an extremely rich diocese he accepted, after first taking the necessary steps to become a priest. Eventually his grandson Cesare Borgia would become Duke of Valencia.

The war for Naples continued between Aragon and France, with Alfonso himself falling into the hands of Filippo Maria Visconti (the walrus we met at the beginning of the book). Visconti was a condottiere fighting for the French and should normally have turned Alfonso over to them, but like Lorenzo *Il Magnifico* de' Medici, Alfonso was so charming that he ended up fascinating the sadistic tyrant, persuading him that it would be better for Milan to have the less powerful Alfonso in Naples rather than the powerful French who, in addition, had ancient claims on Milan. Alfonso was freed just when Martin died. Eugenius, the pope who replaced Martin, had discussions with Alonso Borgia, whom he made a cardinal, and recognized Alfonso's right to Naples. The pope also legitimized King Alfonso's bastard son Ferrante.

Eugenius was replaced by Pope Nicolas, an intelligent, honest, good man who at 49 could have been, in age, Alonso Borgia's son. He confirmed the legitimization of Ferrante. Yet he too died and was replaced--due to infighting between the Orsini and the Colonna--by the last man on earth a bookie would have put his money on, the benign Alonso Borgia himself (called Alonso de Borja at the time), now Pope Calixtus III, age 76.

Calixtus surprised everyone by ordering a crusade against the Turks, but found little following. There had been numerous crusades already, all of which, except the first one, had ended in disaster. A cardinal known as Scarampo was named to head the fleet the pope built with the church's money, but ships promised by Alfonso never materialized, turning Calixtus irredeemably against the man who had set him on the path to becoming pope. He refused to allow King Alfonso to divorce his wife of 40 years and he refused, much more importantly for Alfonso, to ratify the bulls legitimizing his son Ferrante. As I wrote concerning Lorenzo, when he went to Naples he didn't know if Ferrante would kiss him or behead him. This was because Ferrante was a sociopath, the kind only amused by the cruelest butchery. This Calixtus knew because Calixtus, during the years he was the docile Alonso, had been appointed Ferrante's tutor by the man he now hated, Alfonso of Aragon. That Ferrante was a crazed murderer may have been the reason why Calixtus refused to legitimize him, although Alonso also knew that a bastard son would not be allowed to reign by the Spanish, something the Italians accepted without question, something impossible for Spaniards.

Calixtus found help against King Alfonso in strange places. He was aided by an indomitable warrior called Skanderbeg of Albania, so invincible against the Turks that he won Venice's favor, until he became so powerful that Venice feared the dominance of Albania over Venice, and offered a reward for his head. Calixtus was also helped by a character rich in color, known to us today as Dracula, introduced at the beginning of this book. Incredibly, Skanderbeg had been kidnapped by the Turks as a child and had worked his way up through the janissaries until switching sides.

Calixtus, so physically weak he ruled from his bed, followed up he attempt to wage war with the Turks with his decision to take back the Papal States from the lords, dukes, princes and powerful families, like the Colonna and the Orsini, that ruled the countless city-states comprising the Papal States, states that nonetheless belonged to the church situated in Rome. The States were necessary for the glory of the papacy, but also due to their inherent value: fertile flatlands crossed by vital road links to the North and to the Adriatic, an immense source of wealth through taxes and commerce.

For this Calixtus needed men he could count on. As there were none, he turned to boys, namely his sister's sons. One was Pierluigi Borgia, the other Rodrigo Borgia, Rodrigo who, when elected pope, the future Alexander VI, would continue the fight to subdue the Papal States with a boy of his own, his son Cesare. For the moment Calixtus made sure the boys were educated, Rodrigo earning even a doctorate in law, while Pierluigi was named head of the troops headquartered in the Castel Sant'Angelo. Rodrigo was made a cardinal and then Calixtus's own personal aid, known as the vice-chancellor--the most important man in Rome, after the pope--at the unheard-of age of 26. He was also made captain-general over all papal troops--in effect Calixtus's minister of war--a position that put his brother Pierluigi under him. This was accepted by the Colonna and the Orsini because it was through nepotism that they themselves had gained power and prodigious wealth. Pierluigi was then made prefect of Rome, a post that had been held by the Orsini for generations. Pierluigi ventured out from Rome to take back the tiny city-states in the environs, part of the Papal States ruled by the Orsini, earning the hatred of the Orsini for Pierluigi, for Rodrigo and for Calixtus. The Orsini had ruled over Rome and its surroundings like cave-age thugs for a century. Armed, they had taken what they wanted when they wanted it, killing whomever they pleased, having their way with any girl that caught their fancy.

The Colonna were thrilled that Pierluigi had reined in the Osini, and informed him that he could have a Colonna bride whenever he wished. As for Rodrigo, he performed his duties brilliantly, the reason he was so easily accepted by the other cardinals, a master of administration that would be part of the key to his later success as Pope Alexander VI.

Then King Alfonso died, a man of great intelligence, a ruler of vision, a man of unlimited ambition and energy. He would certainly have won over all of Italy had other prodigious figures not appeared at that moment, the Sforza in Milan, the Medici in Florence, popes like Alexander and Julius II in Rome, the Venetians and the Turks. When Calixtus heard of Alfonso's passing he shouted out, "At last free!" As Ferrante hadn't been legitimized, Calixtus simply issued a bull bringing Naples back into the Holy See.

Two things happened next. First, Ferrante moved his army to Naples's borders in preparation for an attack by papal troops and, second, a murderer entered the scene, a fever that had carried off nearly every pope unable to escape to mountain retreats during the summer months of July and August. With Calixtus too ill to move, certain to die, the Orsini took to the streets crying vengeance against all Spaniards, many of whom were killed. Pierluigi was snuck out of the city under disguise and Rodrigo, bravely, remained next to his uncle Calixtus until he rendered his last breath. As said, Rodrigo would be courageous throughout his entire life, no matter the later heinous acts he would be accused of, an indifference to fear that he shared with his son Cesare. As for Pierluigi, he died mysteriously at age 26, poison naturally suspected.

The conclave that followed was set in motion. The Vatican was walled off. The clear winner was thought to be Cardinal d'Estouteville of France, cousin to the King of France and immensely wealthy. On the first vote he received only his own ballot, proof of the maxim: He who enters the conclave pope, leaves a cardinal.

What took place next was pure drama, knowledge of which has come down to us in a document written by the cardinal of Siena, the only time in the history of the church that the contents of a conclave have been divulged. We're told that d'Estouteville offered a part of his wealth to all the cardinals, telling them that the first vote was a fluke, and that he was now but one ballot short of winning. In the secrecy of the latrines, the only private place to talk, he promised something to everyone, assuring Rodrigo that he would continue as vice-chancellor. The cardinal of Siena tells us that he (the cardinal of Siena) was so offended by d'Estouteville's latrine shit that he mounted a counter-offensive. He met with Rodrigo, calling him a "boy" and a "fool" for believing d'Estouteville, assuring him that not only would a Frenchman be the next vice-chancellor, but that the papacy would be moved back to French Avignon.

In the election the next day the cardinal of Siena himself was three votes short of winning. The cardinals decided to meet together in silence until one or several broke it by publically changing his secret vote for oral support. The first to do so was Rodrigo, who declared for the cardinal of Siena. This was followed by another cardinal. Giovanni Colonna, seeing that the cardinal of Siena was certain to win and wanting to cast the critical vote that would swing the election and assure Colonna of the new pope's gratitude, rose to do the same. He was halted by d'Estouteville who tried to drag him out of the room. Colonna nonetheless had time to shout out, "I accede to Piccolomini," making the cardinal of Siena the new pope, Pius II.

G.J. Meyer writes in his wonderful *The Borgia* that Rodrigo had admitted to Pius II that he was going to vote for d'Estouteville for reasons entirely of self-interest. Such candor, says Meyer, "will be characteristic of Rodrigo over the next forty-five years, helping to explain his almost uncanny ability to win the affection of almost anyone who came within his reach." Pius reaffirmed Rodrigo in his function as vice-chancellor, took a fatherly interest in the boy, finding in the already fat Rodrigo someone totally open to Pius's teaching.

Pius was one of 18 children, dirt poor, who studied law. His friends reportedly broke up with laughter when he announced that he was to become a monk, because his joy in the delights of the flesh had already made him the father of several bastards. He was nonetheless religious, walking with a limp caused by a pilgrimage to a shrine of the Virgin, over ice and through snow.

Pius took the waters in Tuscany, from whence he wrote an extraordinary letter to Rodrigo who was back in Siena, stating that Rodrigo had become the laughing stock of Italy owing to his participation in orgies, an example of the pot calling the kettle black, given Pius's own lust and his own sowing of oats when he was Rodrigo's age.

Readers of Robert Caro's monumental life of *LBJ* will recognize a trait Rodrigo and Johnson had in common: both took every position they fought tooth and nail to acquire not only with fanatical seriousness, but developed it into something colossal, milking it for all it was worth. Johnson worked tirelessly to become president, Rodrigo did the same to become pope. Michelangelo had said of himself, "I work harder than any man who has ever lived," and it was true, a truth that could have been applied to Rodrigo Borgia.

Because of continued problems with the Turks, Pius ended the dispute with Naples by declaring Ferrante its new ruler. He then tried to mount a crusade against the Turks but failed when France, whose claim over Naples had been disregarded by Pius, and Venice, who sought peace with the Turks through negotiation, refused to take part. In world history no enterprise suffered more defeats and ended up killing more people--and was a bottomless pit for more money--than the crusades. Christians against Moslems; Christians against Christians, which led even to the sacking of Constantinople by Christians; inhumanity the likes of which have rarely been seen on the face of the earth; acts of horror that have blackened the reputations of kings, like Richard Coeur de Lion, and blackened Christianity itself. Calixtus had failed; and now Pius II would fail too. He set off for Ancona where he planned to see the crusade set sail, only to die, of fever, perhaps bubonic. Rodrigo was stricken too, but survived.

Rodrigo played next to no part of the conclave of 1464 because he was suffering from the aftermath of the Ancona plague. Cardinal Pietro Barbo of Venice was elected, taking the name of Paul II, although originally he had chosen the name Pope Formosus, meaning beautiful, but had been talked out of it, given his sexual bent. Son of Eugene IV through an incestuous coupling with his sister, passed off as Eurgene's nephew, he was made cardinal at age 23. Meyer says he was "tall and handsome ... lived simply and kept himself free of scandal." Most other sources maintain that he spent his life in the company of male prostitutes, rent-boys that he himself, when pope, employed in a carnival that was a nonstop bacchanalia, and that he suffered a heart attack at age 54 while being butt-fucked by his lover, although others maintain that he was being so honored by a favored page.

Paul II kept Rodrigo as vice-chancellor, as did his successor Sixtus IV. Sixtus was the son of a poor fisherman whose title to glory was built on undreamed of nepotism, bringing to Rome a family of fishmongers and appointing, over the papal troops, a boy who had literally been selling fruit on the streets of Liguria when he learned of his uncle's election. Scurrying to Rome the boy quickly rose through the ranks, humping prepubescent girls and marrying into the Sforza of Milan, forcing the hymen of his Sforza bride, Caterina, age 10, with the full consent of Caterina's father whom she adored and who *knew* what was awaiting her (we'll hear *much* more about Caterina later on). In point of fact, Sixtus's family was an early version of Ettore Scola's *The Down and Dirty (Brutti, sporchi et cattivi)*. Sixtus's only success, as far as his family was concerned, was his raising his nephew, the handsome Giuliano della Rovere, to the dignity of cardinal, at age 18. Giuliano would become the future Julius II, arguably the church's most powerful pope ever.

Sixtus had but two objectives in life, destroying the Turks and raising his family to the summits of prosperity, certainly because said family, detecting his intellectual gifts, had pooled their resources to assure the dirt-poor Sixtus's education. Sixtus loved one nephew so much that he was believed to have been both Sixtus's son and his lover, as Sixtus adored boys, one of the reasons for bringing his nephews to Rome. All sources agree that they were louts, yes, but beautiful louts. His son-cum-lover was Pietro Riario. Sixtus turned over bishoprics to the young sire, making him fabulously rich although not enough to cover the boy's debauches, his horse racing, his dissolution. Pietro was a Renaissance man in that he gave himself to both men and women. He was on the most intimate terms with the murderous Galeazzo Maria Sforza of Milan, both eating from the same plate and sleeping in the same bed. The untoward career of the young Pietro ended at age 28--some say due to a fever, others due to indigestion because he adored huge banquets, and still others by poison, soon to become a Borgia specialty--to the incommensurable chagrin of his father/lover Sixtus. Because the pope only trusted his family, the young Pietro was replaced by Girolamo, the lummox who ruptured his wife's hymen at age 10, and named him head of the papal troops. It was the miscreant Girolamo who had had the bright idea of killing Lorenzo, the failure of which had seen Sixtus's handsome nephew and new cardinal--at age 26--Raffaele Riario, taken prisoner.

Sixtus IV

Sixtus did, however, improve Rome by widening the streets and encouraging the construction of new palaces, and by bringing in artists and founding the Sistine Chapel Choir, filling it with beautiful lads.

A discussion of the church is necessary to the understanding of the genesis of Alexander VI. For a time the popes reigned in Avignon, a small pleasant town of beautiful fortifications and two beautiful rivers. They moved back to Rome in order not to lose the Papal States, land held from roughly 500 to 1870 when under Victor Emmanuel II Rome was captured as part of the final unification of Italy (6). The Papal States were expanded under two popes. The first was Alexander VI, whose reign saw the sudden rise of the ultimate warlord, his own son Cesare. The second was Julius II, during whose reign Cesare met his equally sudden end. Both popes had only partial control over the Papal States, their influence varying according to the strength of the lord or count or prince who held this or that papal property.

Depending on the era and the pope, Rome was a dirty town with few inhabitants when compared to ancient times. Much of it was in ruins, the haunt of thieves and murderers, and pastureland filled with goats and sheep. Bands of youths owned the streets, parading where they would, daggers and swords at the ready, beasts with ever-hungry bellies and ever-lustful loins. Cholera and dysentery left corpses where they expired, and the body parts of quartered victims, the remnants of executions, were hammered to doors or, in the case of heads, brandished on pikes. Smelly swamps and piles of refuse polluted the air, a far cry from sweet Avignon.

It was around this time that Rodrigo returned to Spain, the land of his birth, for an extended visit. On his way back his ship was wrecked off the coast of Tuscany and he was taken to Pisa to recover from his close call with death. There, at a banquet in his honor, he met Vannozza de' Catanei, the mother of his future children. In very quick succession she gave him Cesare, Juan, Lucrezia and Jofrè. In return, Rodrigo gave Vannozza a series of complaisant husbands and great wealth. These children were, however, only part of the brood he fathered with other acquaintances. The incredible luck of the Borgia was in having so many offspring, so many boys, boys who survived infancy in times when at least half of all babies died nearly immediately or within a few years of birth. The death toll was so high that even in France, virtually up to modern times, children were given out to wet nurses who cared for them until around age seven, thanks to which parents suffered less when babies they'd rarely seen passed away (and, of course, this left them unburdened from childcare).

When Cesare was eight, Rodrigo moved his brood to the home of his Spanish cousin Adriana da Mila, more qualified to raise them as she was of noble birth and would instruct them in the ways of the aristocracy. Adriana had married into the very powerful Orsini family. Her son married a beauty known as La Bella, whom Rodrigo immediately took as his mistress.

The next pope, Innocent VIII, was known as the Rabbit for his lack of authority. Bands of youths, armed with daggers and swords, ruled the streets of Rome, stealing, raping and murdering to such an extent that the cardinals were forced to place guards with crossbows and artillery at their windows and on the roofs of their palaces. He soon fell ill and died, but not before making Lorenzo *Il Magnifico*'s son Giovanni, age thirteen, a cardinal, a cardinal who would one day become Pope Leo X. The cardinals who came to the Vatican to replace Innocent met in conclave, now decided to elect a strong pope, one who would finally and definitively bring order to Rome, and none was known to be as forceful as Rodrigo Borgia, later suspected of having encouraged the street violence by having his sons Juan and Cesare pay scores of hoodlums to rob, rape and destroy property.

Following the usual bargaining, during which wagonloads of gold, silver, jewels and precious furnishings and tissues were loaded at the Borgia palace and unloaded at the residences of nearly all of the cardinals (a few were said to have refused the bribes), Rodrigo Borgia became Pope Alexander VI. The extent of the bribes will never be known, and anyway, those who ran against him for pope were at least equally wealthy and equally inclined to bribe whomever they could.

49

Rodrigo *was* virile, producing many legitimatized children (as well as being the first pope to ever recognize his bastards), of whom two were to become world famous, a daughter, Lucrezia, and a son, Cesare. He had at least four other children he did not recognize officially, but all his offspring and mistresses were abundantly cared for. Alexander was sensual, fun loving, certainly good to his children, a sugar-daddy papa, extremely tolerant, ruthless, courageous, and an administrator of genius. He also knew the importance of family unity, something far too neglected in children's education, going so far, rumor had it, as to have sexual relations with his daughter and sons Juan and Cesare, but so hated were the Borgia that the truth will never be known. Reporting the accusations, as I'm doing, will keep the rumors alive, not reporting them, even when their origin was the latrines of the concaves, would be a return to the obscurantism of the Middle Ages.

At age 18 Cesare was made a cardinal, causing a howl of outrage among the other cardinals, especially Giuliano della Rovere, the future Warrior Pope Julius II, who would later do his best to see Cesare into an early grave. As mentioned, Alexander had a new mistress known as La Bella. This was Giulia Farnese. Giulia had married Andrea da Mila's son, Orso Orsini (Andrea da Mila was the woman Alexander had chosen to bring up his own children as aristocrats). Giulia had a brother, Alessandro Farnese, that Alexander now made cardinal at the same time as Cesare, again causing great unrest among the cardinals who balked at accepting a boy issued from one of Alexander's mistresses (Andrea da Mila), and the brother of another of his whores (La Bella). At any rate, this was the first step in the rise of the House of Farnese. Alessandro would later become the homosexual Paul III.

Alessandro had been named a cardinal by Alexander VI because he was the brother of Alexander's mistress. The Romans thereby changed his name from Cardinal Farnese to Cardinal Fregnese, "Cardinal Cunt". Once he became Pope Paul III he got his hands on Michelangelo and ordered him to paint *The Last Judgment* in the Sistine Chapel, an immense work that would require scaffolding seven stories high and take five years to finish, longer than Michelangelo had taken on the entire ceiling. In other Last Judgments only the damned were featured naked. Here, nearly everyone was, the saved and canonized alike. As Martin Gayford wrote in his *Michelangelo: His Epic Life*, "nude, curly-haired young men with the bodies of Oympic shot-putters passionately kiss and caress. Some of them hug grey-haired elders." The genitals and asses were later painted over by Michelangelo's assistant, Danielle da Volterra, after his master's death, Volterra's only claim to fame.

CHAPTER FOUR

THE INVASION OF CHARLES VIII
Ludovico Sforza, Gian Galeazzo Sforza, Savonarola, Piero de' Medici, Cardinal della Rovere, Alexander VI, Giovanni Sforza, Cesare, Alfonso II of Aragon, Frederick IV of Naples, Jofrè Borgia, Sancia, Louis XII, Ferrante, Charles VIII

Lorenzo died relatively young from complications probably due to family gout. He turned over the reins to his son Piero who immediately tried to shore up relations with Ludovico Sforza of

Milan, who had succeeded Galeazzo Maria Sforza. Ludovico was known to be devious and unpredictable. He had taken a liking to Lorenzo but Piero lacked his father's charm. Ludovico was in fact a regent for Galeazzo's son Gian Galeazzo, but once he'd gained power Ludovico kept it, a *fait accompli* accepted by Gian Galeazzo who preferred hunting and was considered intellectually stunted. But Gian's wife was Isabella, granddaughter of King Ferrante of Naples, a perfect excuse for Ferrante to send troops to Milan to defend Isabella and Gian Galeazzo's right to the throne, whether Gian Galeazzo liked it or not. Ludovico requested the intervention of France which, due to its constant battles with England, had become the mightiest army at the time. At its head rode Charles VIII. France considered itself the rightful possessor Naples, but also of Milan, which was equivalent to Ludovico inviting a fox into the henhouse. Still, he had no choice, and so it was that two years after Lorenzo's death Charles entered Italy at the forefront of 60,000 men, the greatest invasion since Hannibal.

Savonarola.

The great Guicciardini in his marvelous *Storie fiorentini* tells us more about Savonarola: ''There were no more games in public, and even at home they were played in an atmosphere of fear. The taverns, which had been the meeting places for all the rowdy youth who enjoy every vice, were all closed up. Sodomy was ended and women abandoned showy and lascivious clothing, and young men resolved to live in a saintly and civilized way. They went to church regularly, wore their hair short and cast stones and cursed dishonest men, card players and women who dressed lewdly. They went to the carnival and collected all the dice, cards, paintings and corrupt books, and burned them publicly in the Piazza della Signoria. Savonarola brought help to men who abandoned pomp and vanities, and restricted themselves to the simplicity of a religious and Christian life."

Alexander had a plan of action. He met with Alfonso II's son Ferdinand II who would take troops into the Romagna and stop Charles from entering there. His brother Frederick would sail to Genoa, the destination of Charles's ships. Virginio Orsini promised to keep the French out of the north of Rome, the domain of the Orsini, while Alexander would do the same in the Papal States. But Charles's troops, many of whom were mercenaries, were heat-tempered professions, armed with cannons and the morality of beasts. They plundered, raped and murdered their way south, sending fear into the hearts of men and provoking the complete collapse of Alexander's plan of action. Frederick arrived too late in Genoa so he sailed on to Rapallo. Charles's Swiss mercenaries met him there and sacked and massacred the entire population, after which opposition to Charles in other city-states evaporated.

Charles was well received in Milan where, with his backing, Ludovico had Gian Galeazzo poisoned, although he spread the word that the young man had died from an excess of coitus. Then Charles fell nearly mortally ill with smallpox. When he recovered, his counselors suggested that he take control of Milan where he had been so wonderfully received, reminding him that thanks to marriages in earlier times the French had rights over Milan that were far stronger than those of a simple condottiere like Ludovico, this to the absolute horror of Ludovico himself. But Charles didn't have his mind on either Milan or Naples, really. What he wanted was Jerusalem, having promised God he would liberate the Holy City should he survive the smallpox. He saw himself not only in Jerusalem, but as liberator of Constantinople itself.

Alfonso II fled the city-state of Naples, replaced by his son Ferdinand.

In Florence Lorenzo's son Piero had sided with Naples, earning his expulsion from the city by Florentines who considered

France a far richer market than Naples, a far better client for Florentine banks and manufacturing. This, plus the total destruction of the Florentine garrison of Fivizzano by French troops, tipped the scales against the Medici. Even so, when Charles entered Florence he was coldly received by the people. Piero felt he could make a comeback by seeking out Charles and throwing himself at Charles's feet, offering him free access to the town and, as gifts, Pisa and the port of Livorno. The Pisans were ecstatic because they hated the Florentines with every fiber of their bodies, but when they witnessed the sacking of Pisa and its environs, and the rape of their young girls by Charles's mercenaries, they realized their mistake. Savonarola made his way to Pisa where he welcomed the tyrant, calling him the godsend-liberator he had been predicting in his sermons. In Florence itself Charles told the people, with the breezy candor of his youth, that he cared nothing for them and the leaders they chose to rule them. What he wanted was money, and when he told them the amount they laughed in his face. Furious, Charles shouted that in that case he would sound his trumpets, to which the Florentines countered that they would sound their bell, the bell on the summit of the tower of the Palazzo della Signoria that would bring all the men of Florence and its surroundings running fully armed. Charles, wishing to get on to Naples unhampered, accepted their offer of 120,000 florins.

Before leaving Paris, Charles had entered into a number of extremely expensive treaties with kings such as Henry VII of England in order to cover his back should his engagement in Italy turn out to be more arduous than he had planned. As Naples belonged to the church, Charles needed Alexander's benediction to control it (as did the rulers of the Papal States). But should Alexander prove recalcitrant, Charles was prepared to replace him with the Cardinal della Rovere, the future Julius II, who was at his side, his wish to become pope only equal to his hatred of Alexander. In fact, counselors around the king tried to pursued him that Alexander had bought the papacy and was therefore not legitimate, and that the majority of the cardinals in Rome would thank Charles for rescuing the church by deposing him. Charles's stopover in Rome was the first test of Alexander's exceptional intelligence. Alexander nonetheless thought it a wise precaution to withdraw to the fortified Castel Sant'Angelo with all his possessions, including his bed. Charles tried to calm the Romans by telling them that his army wouldn't take an egg without paying for it. So numerous were his men that they took six hours to file through the gate of Santa Maria del Popolo, Giuliano della Rovere among the entourage. Charles took up residence in the Palazzo Venezia where he sat by the fire in slippers while his food was tasted by servants, his wine tested for poison, and the women sent to him closely inspected by those who knew his preferences. Charles, despite his extreme ugliness, had at least two different women a day, and in his baggage he carried a book of pornographic sketches and paintings of intercourse he had had with a few select beauties. His army may not have stolen a single egg, but it stole everything else that hadn't been battened down, reportedly cutting off fingers when rings refused to budge. His men raped any woman silly enough not to have fled the city. They killed as well, especially the Jews. They took any residence that pleased them, burning the furniture for warmth (Charles entered Rome the 31 of December 1494), leaving the Palazzo Venezia, stated an observer, as dirty as a pigsty. Alexander finally agreed to a meeting that took place in the papal palace. Charles is reported to have rushed to him and was prevented from a third genuflection by the pope who stopped him in mid-kneeling, giving him the kiss of peace on the lips. As Charles and his troops had brought syphilis into Italy, the kiss could not have been hygienic.

Charles VIII.
He never had a woman more than once, and carried a collection of pornography in his baggage.

Syphilis may have been introduced into Europe by Christopher Columbus but this seems questionable as Columbus discovered the Americas in 1492 and the first cases of the disease were recorded in 1494 in Naples during Charles's invasion. How it could have spread so rapidly is one question, another question is why it wasn't present before Charles entered Naples, present in Paris for example. (At that time it was known, in French, as *le mal de Napoli*.) At any rate Charles had it and soon Cesare would be disfigured by its terrible scarification. Charles's embrace of Alexander was an enormous victory for the pope whom Charles was thinking of deposing just a few days earlier, and a temporary defeat for della Rovere.

Alexander successfully bypassed Charles's request that he recognize his claim to Naples, a papal possession, as said, but the French king did insist on having Cesare as a traveling and hunting companion on his way to the city, with its magnificent view of the Bay of Naples and Vesuvius in the background--a hostage to make certain that the pope kept his troops in their barracks. Alfonso II of Naples abdicated in favor of his son Ferdinand II who fled, leaving the city wide-open to Charles. On the way there Cesare hung back with his horse and then took French leave, Charles beside himself with fury. But he ended up forgiving Cesare as the boy had always fascinated Charles. Even in Paris Charles had asked his ambassadors questions about the lad. Cesare apparently could be a heathen when he chose, or charm personified.

Charles had made a mistake in accepting the 120,000 ducats offered by Florentines to get rid of him. This first proof of his fallibility--in tandem with the cruel, inhuman destruction of life and the raping of women--got Milan's Ludovico to thinking that he had made a mistake in inviting him into Italy. He entered into negotiations with Alexander and Venice, his mortal enemy, on how to stop the massacres. The Venetians, extremely well-armed, knew that Charles would eventually move against them, perhaps using their fleets in his plans to invade the Holy Land. As for Ludovico, he was convinced that Charles would finally choose

Milan to conquer over Jerusalem, the reason he solicited the help of Alexander and Venice, along with Siena, Urbino and Bologna, all of whom sent representatives to meet with Alexander.

In face of such unity Charles was forced to retreat from Naples, although his power was intact enough to do grave damage to anti-French coalition sent to fight him, costing the coalition 2,000 men to every 1,000 lost by Charles. The retreating French were nonetheless hounded by troops that attacked their baggage train until nothing remained to Charles of the tons of gold, jewels and other loot he had amassed. He and his Swiss and Gascon mercenaries massacred as they went, wiping Toscanella and Pontremoli off the map. In a way, worse awaited him at Poggibonsi where Savonarola scurried to tell him that he had failed because he hadn't accomplished the will of God; he hadn't cleansed Italy of its filth in the form of the pope and his bastards; he hadn't fulfilled his promise to liberate Jerusalem; and if Charles didn't listen to the word of God that passed through the mouth of his chosen servant Savonarola, God would replace him with someone who would, which the Lord did two years later by fracturing Charles's head against a doorframe as he was rushing off to play tennis, causing him to hemorrhage to death.

As for Alexander VI, he had defeated a king who had had immense wealth and the biggest army of his day, and had given Charles nothing other than the red hat of a cardinal for the king's cousin Philip of Luxembourg.

To say the very least, Alexander hadn't had it easy. He not only had survived under four very difficult popes, he had become pope himself, a Spaniard among Italians--wealthy, aristocratic, well-connected Italians. He had not only held his own among the greatest assembly of leaders known to the world--the Sforza, the Medici, the Orsini, the Colonna and Charles VIII--he had outshone them all. He literally had had nothing other than his intelligence to make him pope, nothing other than that and the ancient prestige of his office to bring them all to heel, eager to kiss his sacred feet and ring. Even Cesare believed in the genius of his father, Cesare who fell to his knees to kiss his feet and hands, as had Charles, and as Louis XII would soon do.

Ferdinand II, Alfonso II's courageous son, was allowed to continue to reign over Naples, and was appointed Duke of Calabria by Alexander in thanks and in gratitude for help during the time of troubles. Ferdinand had gone to the island of Ischia to join his father, after which they went to Sicily where they were joined by Jofrè Borgia and his wife Sancia, ever generous in sharing her charms. At the moment, in fact, she was the mistress of the condottieri Prospero Colonna. They all returned to Naples where they were welcomed by overjoyed crowds, the same that had welcomed Charles a few months before. But it was Charles the eventual winner, leaving behind the French Disease, the *Morbus Gallicus*, syphilis, killing and maiming millions throughout the ages.

Sancia of Aragon

Charles's successor, Louis XII, decided to follow up the ancient French claim to Milan by launching an attack on the city-state. During his invasion Ludovico was captured by Louis and imprisoned in an underground dungeon until his death.

Alexander and Cesare supported the invasion of Louis because Louis, unlike Charles, was intelligent and a man of his word, a man one could make a deal with, a man Alexander and Cesare were convinced he would swing his support, and that of his army, and mercenaries, in favor of Alexander's quest to recover the Papal States as a first move to installing Cesare over the greater part of Italy. It meant, also, Louis' help in the destruction of their enemies, the Orsini and the Colonna, whose hold of the tiny city-states around Rome could choke Rome to death anytime they wished to. In response, Fabrizio and Prospero Colonna allied themselves with Spain, the mortal enemy of the French.

Alexander's idea was to unite the Papal States into an area equivalent in power to Naples, Venice, Florence, Bologna and Ferrara. With the aid of Louis, the reality of such an adventure was at hand, after which would come the reunification of Italy under Cesare, a perilous plan because it meant the eventual expulsion of both the French and the Spanish. Alexander and Cesare started off small, with the seizure of lands belonging to the Gaetani, small-time tyrants who had sided with Naples against Rome and whose lands studded the area around Naples. As for the Colonna and the Orsini, we'll see how father Alexander and son Cesare tried to bring them to heel, strangling some, poisoning others, from the heads of families to an Orsini cardinal. But like dragons' teeth, the Colonna and the Orsini kept springing up from nowhere, and would continue to do so until well after the last of the Borgia.

As said, Savonarola had welcomed Charles with open arms to Florence, claiming that he had asked God to send the Frenchman as an arm to punish the evildoers in Italy in general, and Florence in particular. He had then dismissed the king like a servant. He himself replaced Charles with gangs of boys he sent to scour the city of its whorehouses, its licentious taverns, its musical instruments, its card games and, especially, its sodomists. When Savonarola had first come to Florence he had gained a huge following because he had had the right answers to how Florentines could wage war against corruption, brigands and iniquity. He painted a clear picture of the depravity of the church, from the trade of indulgences to the selling of cardinal hats. He was the precursor of the coming Reformation, and because he was ahead of his time he was burned at the stake--the word of the true God gone up in flames.

Savonarola burned at the stake in Florence and detail, by an unknown artist.

CHAPTER FIVE

THE DEATH OF JUAN BORGIA
Cesare, Jofrè Borgia, Giovanni Sforza, Louis XII, Frederick of Naples, Alfonso of Naples, Juan Borgia, Pedro Calderon

Alexander's children spoke Spanish when together, but they all knew Italian, French and Latin. Cesare was destined for the orders, a destiny he hated as he hated his brother Juan who was marked for a military career, one Juan loved but was not good at--or at least not as good as Cesare would show himself to be. Cesare was described by the great Boccaccio, author of *The Decameron*--a book as wonderful today as then--as possessed of genius and charm, lively and merry and happy in the company of society. He was also ambition to the extreme and fearless--in fact, like his father Alexander, he feared nothing and no one. Cesare addressed Juan as his Lord brother, and admonished him to give thanks to their father His Holiness, who had made the family so great. Juan was married in Barcelona to a young cousin of King Ferdinand and Queen Isabella. Given everything he could wish for from birth, Juan spent his time whoring--and his young body was capable of giving him a great deal of pleasure--drinking and gambling. It's not known if he honored his wife on their wedding night, so decided was he to go off with his friends to shatter the quiet of the Barcelona night. Juan was clearly Alexander's favorite, another supposed reason for Cesare's hatred. As virile as his father, slim waisted and certain of his sex appeal, Juan swaggered through the streets of Rome in what can only be described as gorgeous attire, a black cloak of gold brocade, jewel-encrusted waistcoats and silk shirts, skin-tight trousers with drop-fronts--held in place by ribbons he detached when he wished to piss and fuck. This beautiful, gorgeously clad body, stabbed nine times, 30 golden ducats still in his belt purse, was fished up from the Tiber, to the grief-stricken horror of his father who locked himself away from public view for three days. The death freed the way for Cesare to renounce his vows as cardinal. Alexander never confronted his son with the murder of his favorite boy, but that he was guilty was silently acknowledged by nearly all. On the morning of the murder, just before sunrise, men had been seen leading a horse with a body strapped over its back to the river edge, untie and then cast it into the middle. They were accompanied by another man on a white charger, his silver stirrups and gold spurs reflecting the moon's glow. The men, said the witness, a Slovenian watchman standing guard over boats carrying cargo, spoke in very low voices ... in Spanish. So it was Cesare the murderer ... unless ... unless, thought some, it was his other brother, Jofrè.

It's not clear at exactly what age Jofrè married but he was thought to be 12 and his wife Sancia 16. As puberty was far later in the Renaissance than today (possibly as late as ages 15 or 16) he was unwilling to consummate the union, his testosterone levels too low to inspire the necessary lust. His brothers took over the task for him, however, an experience that was not necessarily grueling for the young girl as she was rumored to have had many lovers before arriving in Rome. At any rate, some historians place their bet on Jofrè as his brother's assassin, out of jealously, Juan who had taken Jofrè's place on Jofrè's wedding night, to the joy of Sancia who loved his slim virile body, and so close were the brothers that it is not impossible that Jofrè was present, Juan demonstrating what would be expected of him later. With puberty came the realization of the extent to which Juan had made a fool of him, a secret that should have remained between the brothers but one that Juan couldn't help bragging about, the consequence of which was Jofrè's hatred for the warrior brother he had until then worshipped. Yet in reality, Jofrè played only a minor role in the uncoiling events attached to the Borgias. He was made Prince of Squillace, a vassal town of Naples where he lived until he died, having produced four children of his own. Jofrè seems to have been a loving prince, certainly a lucky one as he was the center of attention in Squillace, attended by scores of servants, and for a boy who was so calm and steady, a wife like Sancia may have added spice to his otherwise tranquil existence.

Cardinal Ascanio Sforza was also suspected of killing Juan as he had had a clash with the boy for unknown reasons, although few reasons were necessary for the headstrong Juan to pick fights with everyone, a clash that may have ended up with men fighting for and against Ascanio, and Juan killed in the scuffle, the natural end of a boy who thrived on violence.

Others thought the murderer was Lucrezia's husband Giovanni Sforza. After the marriage, Giovanni learned that his wife had had sexual congress with both her brothers Cesare and Juan, as well as her father Alexander, or so it was rumored, rumors gaining in lewdness with each retelling. Giovanni wished to destroy them all, as a way of avenging his humiliation at having been made a fool of. Again, the accusations of incest were based on nothing more than rumors, and as Sabatini had put it so well, historians were ready to accept any nonsense as long as it was "well-salted and well-spiced". (Alas, there is no adequate painting of Juan.)

Despite the fact that Cesare had murdered his brother and Alexander's favorite son, Juan, both father and the remaining son, Cesare, now formed an alliance, the purpose of which was to extend Alexander's power and to give Cesare enough strength so that he would be able to replace the pope, at his death, becoming the first ruler of a unified Italy since the Romans.

To get things going, Alexander had arranged a rapprochement between Louis XII of France and the Vatican. This the pope accomplished thanks to three of the new king's needs: the need to conquer Milan, his possession due to a grandmother who had married a Visconti, one of Milan's first rulers; the need to reconquer Naples, lost with the death of Charles VIII; and the need for a divorce so that Louis could marry Charles's widow. Louis offered Alexander a huge sum of money and gave Cesare, whom all recognized as the new rising star, the duchy of Valence. Cesare would also be given command over several thousand French troops. Satisfied, Alexander threw in a cardinal's hat that the French had requested for years. Not to be outdone, Louis raised the stakes by offering to find Cesare a noble wife. Alexander's rapprochement paid off in spades. Thanks to French intervention in Italy, the four greats would be neutered: Florence and Bologna would become client states of France, doing Louis' bidding in exchange for his protection against Cesare; Venice would be neutralized by the offer of some territorial scraps when Louis conquered Milan; and Milan itself would be French.

When Cesare realized that he would soon be meeting Louis in person, he decided to turn himself into a perfect male by force of exercise, physical exercise as well as exercise in arms and horsemanship. He spent hours at the task and contemporaries agreed that there was not a finer looking Italian in all of Italy, with the exception of Astorre Manfredi who began to attract artists and sculptors to Faenza to capture his face for eternity. The artists who flocked to do Astorre honor wielded an art that was reborn, one that took its roots in humanism and in classical antiquity. It was based on classical texts rediscovered thanks to the likes of Cosimo de' Medici and thanks to commissions by powerful popes, cardinals, tyrants, dukes and kings. It was accompanied by technical advances that improved the quality of oil-paint adopted by Titian, Tintoretto and Uccello. Da Vinci perfected the art of painting thanks to lighting and perspective, as well as incredible detail in anatomy and landscapes. At the same time, the church decided that a man's body, modeled after Christ's own, could not be considered, in modern terms, pornographic, the result of which is the immense number of nudes in paintings found in cathedrals, and nude statuary that decorated palaces, especially those of wealthy cardinals.

As for Lucrezia, Alexander had given her to Giovanni Sforza for husband, but discovering that the boy was a spy for Milan, Alexander decided to annul the marriage in favor of Alfonso of Aragon, a member of the royal family of Naples and also Sancia's brother (the promiscuous wife of Alexander's son Jofrè). After the slaying of Juan, Giovanni feared that Cesare would kill him too in order to further the ties between the Borgia and Naples. So he easily accepted the annulment, especially when he was told that he didn't have to reimburse Lucrezia's dowry of 31,000 ducats. He nonetheless spread the rumor that Alexander wanted the annulment so he could have Lucrezia for himself, and he bruited the rumor that he knew for a fact that Cesare had enjoyed his sister on many occasions. When Alexander informed him that he would have to sign a statement saying that he was impotent, he answered that he had had Lucrezia a thousand times. As an additional proof of her innocence, Lucrezia was examined and found to be *vergo intacta*. In reality she was six months pregnant and would give birth to a boy, financially endowed by Alexander.

Lucrezia's first husband Giovanni Sforza. In his mid-twenties, he took Lucrezia's virginity at age 13 with Sforza brutality, brutality visible in this excellent painting of him.

The boy responsible for her pregnancy was a handsome Spanish valet, Pedro Calderon. Lucrezia most probably had many lovers who were dear to her, but this boy she'd freely chosen, for whom her love must certainly have been deep. Yet he was a commoner, unfit to have fathered the son of a Borgia, even if they were all themselves bastards. Cesare, in a frenzy of rage, chased him through the palace until the lad sought shelter within the robes of Alexander VI. The pope tried to protect him but Cesare slashed at the boy through the robes, literally cutting him to pieces, splattering Alexander's hands and face. The body was cast into the Tiber, his brother Juan's watery tomb, and would be, in a few years' time, the final resting place of Astorre Manfredi, slain also by Cesare, also thrown into the Tiber, tied to that of his brother.

Cesare, as cardinal, had been chosen by his father to crown Frederick of Aragon, King of Naples and, at the same time, convince Frederick to give his son to Lucrezia, still only 18, for husband. Alfonso's son was 17-year-old Alfonso of Aragon, Sancia's brother (Sancia who was Alexander's son Jofrè's wife and certainly the deceased Juan's mistress, as well as Cesare's, and was said to have loved Cesare to the extent of wanting him for husband). At the same time, Cesare hinted that he wouldn't mind marrying King Frederick's daughter. As his son Alfonso was illegitimate, Frederick felt he could marry Lucrezia, but as his daughter was legitimate, there was no question of her marrying syphilitic Cesare, a bastard even if his father was pope. At any rate the daughter, Carlotta, was in love with another, something that would normally not have stopped Frederick from doing what he wanted with her, but the girl held firm, the stars were in her favor, and she finished with the boy she loved. During his stay in Naples, Cesare was said to have fallen for the daughter of the Conte d'Aliffe, on whom he spent 200,000 ducats.

Jofrè Borgia – Too young to satisfy Sancia, Cesare and Juan did so in his place.

Alfonso 17, Lucrezia's second husband. She was 18 and was thought to have sincerely loved him.

Alfonso and Lucrezia were joined in matrimony, and the marriage was consummated.

During the union of nobles, a boy and a girl's fathers often sat beside the nuptial bed, in amiable conversation to be sure of penetration. At times a boy of even fifteen was inoperative because his body simply didn't produce the testosterone that gave him a sufficient level of lust. In this case, the boy and girl would simply giggle, naked, side by side. The consequences of the absence of observers could be disastrous, as in the case of Henry VIII who wanted a divorce from Catherine of Aragon. A papal dispensation had allowed Henry to marry Catherine of Aragon who had been Henry's brother's bride for six months before he died, leaving Catherine a virgin as he had been too ill to be operative--although the day after the wedding he'd bragged to his friends, "Last night I visited the depths of Spain." But there had been no witnesses to the penetration. The refusal of the Warrior Pope Julius II to allow the divorce would end Catholicism in England, all because Henry wanted to reign supreme and fuck his way through five additional wives.

CHAPTER SIX

LOUIS XII
Cesare's syphilis, his marriage to Carlotta of Navarre, the murder of Alfonso, Pietro Torrigiano, the Romagna, the Malatesta

Once Cesare had prepared his body in advance of his trip to France where he would meet Louis XII and the bride Louis was seeking for him, his remaining worry was his face, perhaps not equal to the beauty of Astorre's, but his good looks were increasingly disfigured by the ravages of syphilis. The syphilitic rashes, euphemistically called "flowers", came and went like the tide, leaving him handsome or disfigured *selon*. He took to wearing masks during his bad days, the effect of which enhanced the fear people already had of him.

When the time came, Cesare set off for France with cartloads of precious gifts. He was beautifully dressed in black velvet, pearls and gold chains and precious gems attached to his clothes and boots, his horse attired in gorgeous livery and silver bells, his spurs as gold and polished as witnessed when he was seen at the Tiber disposing of the body of his brother. He was accompanied by dozens of mules covered in satin and cloth of gold, dozens of grooms in crimson velvet, noblemen in gold and silver, trumpeting musicians, all of which, stated chroniclers, had the French laughing at his pomposity. He knelt to kiss Louis' foot but was halted and allowed the king's hand instead. In addition to the wealthy display, Cesare had not forgotten the cardinal's hat to be presented to Georges d'Amboise, Louis' trusted counselor. Cesare was offered the sister of the King of Navarre for wife, sixteen-year-old Carlotta. Alexander was hoping for a better match for his son, a girl from the king's own family, but allowed the marriage because Cesare seemed happy with her. It was, in reality, a match Louis had fought to conclude, as Carlotta was, after all, a princess, while Cesare was still an obscure Italian, and a bastard at that, although Alexander VI tried to help things along by throwing in a cardinal's hat for Carlotta's brother, Amanieu d'Albert. Louis wrote Alexander a description of the wedding night, telling the pope that Cesare honored his wife eight times in a row. Louis added that he had done the same with his new wife--thanks to the divorce Alexander had accorded him--but confessed that he had nonetheless done less well as his sessions had been broken up, twice before dinner, six times afterwards. Alexander replied that he was awed by the king and proud of his son but not surprised by his virility. Carlotta was immediately pregnant with a girl, Cesare's only known child. Charles's former wife wasn't. As for Louis' first wife, she entered a nunnery and was canonized in 1950. From here on, Cesare would put the French coat-of-arms, the fleur-de-lys, on all his possessions, accompanied by the Borgia bull.

Cesare's coat-of-arms with the French fleur-de-lys and Borgia bull.

Cesare rode with Louis to Lyons where the king remained, it being forbidden for a king to enter combat without a male heir, but later Louis joined Cesare in Milan when it was safe for him to do so, accompanied by cardinal della Rovere (who was now following Louis as he had followed Charles VIII, still hoping to replace Alexander as pope). They visited Leonardo's *The Last Supper* in the convent of Santa Maria delle Grazie, the paint already beginning to flake.

Now that Alexander and Cesare were aligned with France against Milan and Naples, Lucrezia's new husband Alfonso, illegitimate son of the former king of Naples Alfonso II, was an embarrassment that the two men eliminated by eliminating Alfonso himself. That Lucrezia loved the boy was no obstacle. Alfonso had dined with the pope and was on his way home when waylaid by men with daggers. Wounded, he was taken to the Vatican where Alexander gave him his own rooms. Instinctively knowing what was in store for the lad, Lucrezia hovered over him day and night, as did Alfonso's sister Sancia. Alfonso knew who was responsible for his injuries, and when he had recuperated enough, he took a potshot at Cesare with a crossbow as he passed through the garden below Alfonso's window. Cesare was unscathed, but his reaction was immediate. He sent men to clear Alfonso's rooms of both Alfonso's sister, Sancia, and his wife, Lucrezia. When they refused to budge, the men told the women they were acting under orders from the pope himself, and, if the two women doubted their word they could ask the pope who was in an adjoining apartment. As they left to do so, the doors to Alfonso's chambers were closed and Alfonso strangled, probably by Micheletto, Cesare's henchman. Cesare made no pretense of innocence, maintaining that since Alfonso had tried to kill him, he was only protecting his life.

Cesare then left Rome at the head of thousands of French troops and headed for the Romagna and the city-states he was set on conquering in the name of the pope because they were, after all, Papal States. On his way he visited his dear sister Lucrezia who was recuperating at Nepi after the loss of her beloved Alfonso. One wonders what they could possibly have had to say to each other.

One of the men accompanying Cesare was the artist Pietro Torrigiano. His story is singular in that Torrigiano had been a sculptor under the patronage of Lorenzo *Il Magnifico*. He is credited with bringing the artistic segment of the Renaissance to England where he finished out his life. But through a quirk of human nature, he is known today as the man who broke the nose of Michelangelo. Torrigiano had been one of Michelangelo's lovers and, in a fit of jealousy, smashed the great artist in the face. Knowing how furious Lorenzo would be at his disfiguring Michelangelo, Torrigiano fled. As Cesare was offering money to new conscripts, and as Torrigiano needed money, he joined his troops. Later he would become renowned for sculpting the memorial to Henry VII of England, a man as atypical as Torrigiano (see Chapter Twelve).

Torrigiano wasn't the only person in need of money. To help finance Cesare's wars in the Romagna Alexander sold 13 new cardinal hats to the highest bidder, raking in 160,000 ducats.

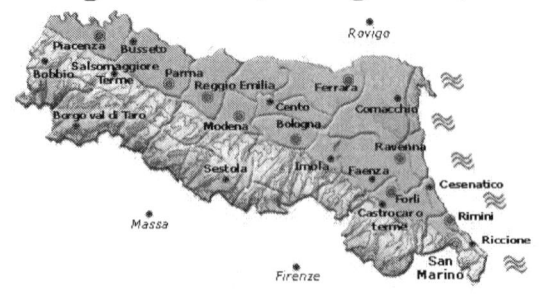

The Romagna.
A region originally held by Gauls, it was taken over by Rome, its name meaning ''land inhabited by Romans''. It was ceded to the Papal States in 1278 and held by very divisive lords, especially the Ordelaffi and the Malatesta, a perpetual battleground, a land of plenty and a land of massacres.

From Nepi Cesare went on to Rimini to capture the city-state from the Malatesta. The Malatesta were a family of hotheads, schemers and murderers who ruled Rimini from 1295 until the arrival of Cesare Borgia who extinguished them with the ease of blowing out a candle. The first Malatesta was a hunchback, Giovanni (ca. 1240 – 1304), called Giovanni the Lame, who killed his wife Francesca and his brother Paolo when he discovered them in *flagrante delicto*:

Francesca and Paolo by Ingres.
The story of her believing that she had been bedded by Paolo, and not Giovanni, may not have been true, but her affair with Paolo, her husband's brother, was.

Paolo was called *"Il Bello"* and his affair with Francesca had been going on for ten years. The great writer Boccaccio claims that Francesca's father had favored the marriage as a way of favoring good relations between his family and the Malatesta, but fearing that Francesca would refuse Giovani, a cripple, he had her believe that she would be wedding the far more handsome Paolo, and that it was only following the wedding night, after she had surrendered her virginity to the boy she loved, that she discovered the ruse, that the man in her bed was Giovanni, a perfect story *à la Boccaccio.*

The murdered Paolo had a son, Ramberto. He was contacted by a cousin, Uberto, who wanted to kill Pandolfo I Malatesta, Lord of Rimini, and take over his lands. But Uberto was the son of Giovanni Malatesta, Giovanni the Lame, the murderer of Ramberto's father. In the finest Italian tradition of treachery, Ramberto invited Uberto to a banquet to finalize plans for the murder, but it was Uberto himself the main course.

Ramberto then planned to gain total power by eliminating two other Malastesta, Malatesta II and Ferrantino Malatesta. As a banquet had worked so well the first time, he organized a second, inviting both cousins. Ferrantino showed up but Malatesta II couldn't make it. Ferrantino was made prisoner, escaping death until Malatesta II could be imprisoned too. But Malatesta II came with an army. He freed Ferrantino and forced Ramberto to flee.

Ferrantino's son, Malatesta Novello, understood what no other member of the family seems to have been able to comprehend, that Ramberto and his plots and intrigues would only stop with the death of Ramberto himself. So Malatesta Novello invited Ramberto to a banquet of his own where he plunged a knife into Ramberto's neck, but not before giving his uncle time to beg for his precious life.

Sigismondo Pandolfo Malatesta (1417 – 1468) was called the Wolf of Rimini. A fearless condottiere, he was also a poet and patron of the arts. He began his conquests at age 13 against Carlo II Malatesta who wanted to annex Rimini. He took over Carlo's lands and became lord of Rimini at age 15. He later gained Pesaro by defeating his own brother Malatesta Novello. He married

Ginevra d'Este but had her poisoned when a better match offered itself, that with Polissena Sforza. He fought for the pope and then against him, for Naples and then against it, for the Sforza and then against them, this last treason ending in the death of his wife Polissena whom he had ordered his servants to drown like a cat.

He had a number of sons from a huge variety of mistresses, one of whom was beheaded by her husband, Rodolfo Gonzaga, when he found out. His third wife was Isotta degli Atti, his longtime mistress. He was accused by Pope Pius II of incest with one of his sons, Roberto. The pope sent a fifteen-year-old priest, the Bishop of Fano, to notify him of his excommunication for incest and a number of treasons. He publicly sodomized the boy-bishop in the square of Rimini, in front of his applauding troops. Sodomy was such a Renaissance pastime that the Germans called it *Florenzer*, anal sex *à la Florentine*

In Rome a procedure called the canonization into Hell was brought against Sigismondo. In an unprecedented ceremony--not repeated since--he was sent to hell and its eternal flames. His image was burned in public and war was declared against him by a league encompassing the pope, the King of Naples and the Dukes of Milan and Montefeltro. He defeated them all except for Federico da Montefeltro, the greatest condottiere to have perhaps ever lived, who took Sigismondo's land that he later returned to the pope and the Papal States, leaving Sigismondo only Rimini.

The great historian Francesco Guicciardini described Sigismondo as an enemy of "the peace and peace lovers," a man who lived for intrigue and duplicitous dealings, in that sense a veritable Renaissance Italian, coupled with the fact that he went from men to women and back with total abandon. He attempted to justify the "disorders" in his life in sonnets to his third wife, Isotta.

He ended as a highly respected condottiere under Venice. Rimi went to his son Sallustio after his death, but was recuperated by the son he had sodomized, Roberto.

Roberto, the victim of his father Sigismondo's incest, was a fearless condottiere, smart enough to align himself with the great Federico da Montefeltro and win back Rimini from his father's designated heir, Sallustio, son of Sigismondo's beloved mistress and then wife Isotta. He made peace with Isotta and his two half-brothers, Sallustio and Valerio, and, in the Malastesta family tradition, threw a banquet for them all during which he poisoned them. Years later Machiavelli in his *The Prince* would write that this was the only possible way for a ruler to deal with his competition, that his choice was between the extinction of potential rivals or his own extinction later one.

Pope Sixtus IV confirmed Roberto as Lord of Rimini and, more importantly, Federico da Montefeltro--who possessed the real power in the region--gave him his daughter. Once this was all accomplished Roberto up and died of malaria. His son Pandolfo took his place until forced to flee Rimini before the advancing troops of Cesare Borgia, thusly ending the line of the Malatesta.

On his way back from Rimini Cesare came upon the sister of the ruler of Rimini whom he had just chased from power, the grandson of Sigismondo. Cesare immediately sequestered and raped her over a period of months, denying any knowledge of her whereabouts. Anyway, he scoffed, he didn't need to rape women as they came to him willingly from everywhere. Which was true. Ambassadors from many city-states were nonetheless so upset by the abduction that they joined forces in demanding that Alexander severely punish his son. Alexander too was reported as being upset, but in the end, what could he do? The woman was eventually restored to her husband but from what she reported later, either she was suffering from Stockholm syndrome or her months with Cesare hadn't been all that traumatizing.

Niccolò Machiavelli will soon enter into our story. But for the moment let's satisfy ourselves with his observations of what the Romagna consisted of. Machiavelli explains that the Romagna was the worst nest of criminals in all of Italy. Murder, rape and theft were daily events, and the princes or lords or counts who ruled did so only to enrich themselves. The soil of the Romagna was excellent and if the lawlessness could have been brought under control, says Machiavelli, and the area united, it would have had more power than Venice or Florence or Milan or Bologna. This was the objective of Pope Alexander VI, a unified region from which his son Cesare would venture out to conquer all of Italy, a first step in uniting it into one country.

CHAPTER SEVEN

CATERINA SFORZA
Galeazzo Maria Sforza, Girolamo Riario, Sixtus IV, Astorre Manfredi, Antonio Ordelaffi, Ravaldino, Bishop Savelli, Ottaviano Riario, Galeotto Manfredi, Lorenzo *Il Magnifico*, Pope Innocent VIII, Erasmus, the Gutenberg Press, Alfonso d'Este, Alexander VI, Giacomo Feo, Giovanni de' Medici

Caterina Sforza now makes her entry into our story. That she was illegitimate was of no consequence in the Italy of the Renaissance. In that, Italy was exceptional. Not only was Caterina treated with the same love as her legitimate brothers and sister, she was offered the same education as the boys in the palace, unlike what girls could expect in most other parts of the country. In addition to a superb education, she learned to handle arms, to ride and to hunt. She was a Sforza, born into a family of warriors that dated back to Francisco Sforza, her grandfather. She was thusly the daughter of Francisco Sforza's son, Galeazzo Maria Sforza, whom she adored, and the mother she loved, Lucrezia Landriani. Caterina was destined to be married three times and through each marriage she would proudly wear the Sforza name, Sforza meaning "force" in Italian. Her love for her father continued untainted even when, at age ten, she was betrothed to Girolamo Riario, count of Imola, who insisted on deflowering her despite the tradition that girls should be at least fourteen. Girolamo had been offered another girl, age eleven, but her family backed out as soon as they learned of Girolamo's pedophilic tendencies. You may remember that Girolamo was the nephew of Pope Sixtus, a fruit seller Sixtus had taken off the streets to make head of his troops, as well as count of Imola and Forlì. Like all of Sixtus's "nephews", he may also have been Sixtus's son and lover. Girolamo was universally described by contemporary historians as being deprived without, alas, further details--

although the reason may simply have been his taste for virgins and a huge capacity for women in general. Caterina's wedding night may have been rough (as her beloved father certainly *knew* it would be), but thereafter she was known for her numerous sexual encounters and her attraction to especially handsome lads, one of whom, a stable boy, she raised to lord of Forlì after her husband Girolamo's death. She would eventually present Girolamo with six sons and a daughter.

Girolamo Riario hated the Medici with every bone in his body because they had always been obstacles in every adventure initiated by the Riario. He therefore tried to assassinate Lorenzo *Il Magnifico* and his brother Giuliano, as we've seen. Girolamo would become known for his cowardliness in battle, and here too, in the attempt on Lorenzo's life, he was not to be found in the heat of things. Only the confessions of the perpetrators made it clear to all of Italy the essential role that had been his in the plot.

In rapid succession she had two sons, Ottaviano, whose godfather was none other than Cardinal Rodrigo Borgia, and Cesare, named after the great Roman, he who crossed the Ribicon, a river just a short distance from Forlì.

Between Imola and Forlì was the city-state of Faenza, home of the Manfredi, the birthplace of Astorre Manfredi. Imola, Forlì and Faenza were part of the Papal States, territories under the sovereignty of the pope, and represented his temporal power on earth. Popes had only partial control over the States, some of which were under the command of princes. The hold over Faenza by the Manfredi was backed by the Este family of Ferrara, a country to the north of Faenza, too powerful for the current pope to bring into the Papal States. The power in Forlì, on the other hand, had gone from despot to pope and back again for centuries. At the moment it was ruled by the Ordelaffi.

Antonio Ordelaffi had come to power in Forlì thanks to Venice. Forlì was a well-fortified city surrounded by walls and surmounted by the nearby fortress of Ravaldino, which controlled passage between the north and south of Italy, as well as roads entering the Apennines. The city was passed on to Antonio's son Francesco who was murdered by his brother Pino. Pino failed to take Machiavelli's advice in such cases, he exiled Francesco's small sons instead of strangling them as did the Turks their brothers and brothers' sons. He then went on to poison his wife whom he suspected of infidelity. As she had been born in neighboring Faenza, he gained the enmity of the Manfredi. He next poisoned his second wife and his second wife's mother, both from Imola, gaining him the hatred of the Imolesi. His third bride, Lucrezia Mirandola, was said to carefully watch what she ate. He had no children from any of his wives but did produce a bastard whom he named to succeed him when he fell ill. So hated was he by even his own Forlivesi that he was pulled from his sick bed, still breathing, and thrown over the balcony of his palace to the streets below, along which his body was dragged, spat upon and kicked until unrecognizable.

His wife Lucrezia became regent for Pino's son but Francesco's boys, now youths, returned to take power. They easily captured the city but not the adjoining fortress, Ravaldino, a fortress that would play an important part, later, in the story of Caterina Riario Sforza de' Medici herself. It was within Ravaldino that Lucrezia and her son took refuge. But the boy mysteriously died, giving Pope Sixtus IV the excuse he needed to send in Caterina's husband Girolamo. Girolamo's army chased the three youths from Forlì and now both Forlì and Imola belonged to him and Caterina, count and countess, but not the fortress of Ravaldino. Because it was unbreachable, Pope Sixtus offered Lucrezia 139,000 ducats and a new castle if she would leave, which she gladly did.

Caterina and Girolamo visited their new acquisition, a backwater in comparison to Rome (which was, compared to Florence, a slum). The inhabitants were awed by the noble dress of the royal couple, their beautiful horses, the trumpets, flags, banners and pennants that accompanied their displacements.

The only jewel remaining to complete Girolamo's diadem was Faenza, the city-state lying between Forlì and Imola. Famous for its ceramics (faience, ergo the name Faenza) and bricks (from which Ravaldino was constructed), it was a land of vineyards and fertile valleys. At the moment Faenza was ruled by Galeotto Manfredi who had the support of his neighbor to the north, Ferrara, ruled by Ercole d'Este. Galeotto's wife was also the daughter of the lord of Bologna. Although Ferrara was an influential city-state and Ercole a condottiere, the powers of the region were clearly Milan, Florence, Venice and Bologna. Faenza and its ruler Galeotto Manfredi were therefore backed by Ferrara and its condottiere Ercole d'Este; by Bologna and the Bentivoglio family, whose daughter was Galeotto's wife; and Florence, ruled by Lorenzo *Il Magnifico*, who would have been glad to stick a dagger into Girolamo's throat because of his role in Lorenzo's brother's death. Girolamo's only support was Sixtus IV, obliging him to renounce, for the time being, the seizure of Faenza.

Little by little Girolamo became unpopular in both Forlì and Imola. When he first arrived he had freed both states from paying taxes, but soon he found himself near bankruptcy. He persuaded the citizens to vote money to fund 400 guards while in reality he had only 100; he pocketed the difference, an embezzlement that soon came to light. He was haughty and known to swap dirty jokes with his guards in the middle of mass in church.

In Rome he was even more unpopular. Everyone knew of Sixtus's nepotism. Girolamo, the shoemaker's boy, had been named head of the papal guards and six other nephews had received cardinals' hats. All were profligate, one spending, in a very short period, the equivalent of what the war against the Turks cost Sixtus. Old Roman families detested Girolamo's boorish ways and pretention. Only Caterina lived up to what the people expected from a countess and the pope adored her for it. Girolamo, in his soul a thug, knew that the pope had little time left to him. He therefore did everything he could to steal anything he could get his hands on, and send it back to Forlì and Imola. Girolamo sold church offices and demanded money from those employed by the church so that they could keep their jobs. The people knew he was a coward because of his role in the death of Lorenzo's brother, and even during the plague in Forlì and Imola, where Caterina had gone from hovel to hovel to bring comfort and priests and what medicines were available to the sick, Girolamo remained in quarantine in his palace, although he did send others, notably his wife, to bring help to the needy.

As Sixtus approached the end, Girolamo put his children into carts filled with furniture, clothing and all the money that hadn't already been expedited, and made his way back to the sticks--Forlì and Imola. The pope's last breath was the signal for his palace and the palaces of his supporters to be ransacked by mobs of the discontented who stole or destroyed what they could, killing nobles foolish enough to attempt to stop them.

Incredibly, Caterina didn't flee. She seized Castel Sant'Angelo in the center of Rome, while her husband had long since vanished through the city gates.

The Castle Sant'Angelo was so named by the Orsini pope Nicholas III when he saw the Archangel Saint Michael hovering over the summit. Built by Hadrian (2) and known for centuries as Hadrian's Mausoleum, other emperors followed Hadrian into its stubby walls. Exactly like the tower of London, it was a residence, a prison, a site for torture and murder, and an impregnable fortress used in times of dire need.

Sant'Angelo

As head of the papal forces, Girolamo had received orders from Sixtus to defend Castel Sant'Angelo at all costs. Instead, Girolamo had run away, leaving Catherine who declared that Girolamo was still responsible for the Castel until the election of the next pope. This was not possible, however, because the Castel guarded the entrance to the papal palace where the next pope would be named, and Caterina proclaimed that her cannons would blow up anyone trying to get past them. To end the imbroglio, the College of Cardinals decided to offer Girolamo, by the intermediary of Caterina, 8,000 ducats if she would to give up her hold over them. The College also promised that Girolamo would have continued lordship over both Forlì and Imola as long as he and his descendants lived. For these reasons Caterina agree to evacuate the Castel.

Back in Forlì Caterina found life there and in Imola boring and dangerous, the weather dreadfully cold and humid. Taddeo Manfredi, who had once ruled Imola, tried, unsuccessfully, to get the town to revolt against its new masters. Both towns were furious over new taxes and duties and both were near bankruptcy. In March the former ruler of Forlì, Antonio Ordelaffi, sent an assassin to kill both Girolamo and Caterina, a plot discovered in time. The assassin was hanged outside the window of the Girolamo palace as a warning to the citizens of both towns, nearly all of whom now despised Girolamo. Worst still for the population, a new outbreak of plague appeared, giving Caterina another chance to help the needy while Girolamo remained locked inside his rooms, forbidding entrance to anyone.

To change air, Caterina decided to visit her mother, sister and relatives in Milan. There, to her stupefaction, she found a city in full bloom thanks to Ludovico Sforza who had opened Milan to engineers, architects and artists. In fact, the city was being rebuild from the foundations up. The most famous Sforza acquisition was the young Leonardo da Vinci whom everyone found gorgeous-- slim, strong, physically powerful and possessing cascades of hair flowing around his beautiful face. Caterina anticipated a close relationship by offering the boy a commission to do her portrait. Alas for her, this boy preferred other boys.

Back home in Forlì, Caterina became more and more aware of her husband's unpopularity. Things finally boiled over, and what Caterina had expected happened: One of the noble clans, the Orsi, decided to use the disgust for Girolamo in an attempt to gain control of Imola and Forlì. As close friends of his, they were allowed to enter the palace early one afternoon while Girolamo was resting, and knifed him. Girolamo was able to raise himself and attempted to get to Caterina's rooms but the Orsi brothers kept slashing with daggers until he lay in a pool of his own blood. The body was thrown over the balcony into the piazza where Forlivesi examined the mangled remains and bloody face. At first fearful, they turned on it once they knew the tyrant was truly dead. He was kicked, spat upon and beaten. The Forlivesi then sacked the palace, taking away everything, down to the bedding. The Orsi ran to Caterina's apartments where she was entertaining her mother, sister and children. The children broke into terrified sobs, except for Girolamo's bastard son Scipione, age 14, who faced the attackers with bravado until unarmed. They were all locked in but luckily Caterina was able to get a message out to Naples and Bologna, as well as to the new pope, Innocent VIII in Rome. Bishop Savelli, who happened to be touring the region, entered Forlì the next day and immediately, on learning what was going on, went to make sure that nothing had happened to Caterina and her children. As the population knew that she could count on the huge armies of both Milan and Bologna, neither it nor the Orsi dared harm her. In addition, the mighty fortification of Ravaldino was in the hands of a man loyal to the countess.

Whether Bishop Savelli was in league with Caterina or not is unknown. What is known is that he accompanied her to the fortification of Ravaldino that she promised to hand over to the Orsi. The keeper, following prearranged instructions, said he would lower the drawbridge if Catherine paid his back wages and ensured his future employment there or elsewhere. When she agreed, he said she would have to enter the fortification and give him what he wanted in writing. The Orsi rejected the idea until Bishop Savelli vouched for her integrity. She entered Ravaldino, the door closed behind her, she mounted the steps to the top of the tower where she gave the Orsi--the finger.

The Orsi, outraged, went back to the palace where they fetched her oldest son Ottaviano, age nine. He was brought back before the walls of Ravaldino and a dagger was placed against the terrified lad's throat, the worst possible nightmare for a mother. The child was obliged to cry out for mercy, alerting Caterina to his presence. She returned to the top of the tower and stared down at the Orsi, their troops and the town people who had desecrated the body of her husband and ransacked her palace. She felt she had little to fear as they were all deathly afraid of the consequences of their acts. Spies had already returned to Forlì to inform them that troops from Bologna and Milan were on the way, and they all knew too that the new pope would never accept that even a hair of any of the children be harmed. Accordingly, Caterina hollered out the words that have made her famous to this day. She told them all that they could do what they would with her children as she was pregnant again and with *this*, she added, pointing to her loins, she could produce many others. Duly impressed, Ottaviano was returned to the care of Bishop Savelli.

Caterina's stance at Ravaldino had a highly unforeseeable consequence. Antonio Maria Ordelaffi, whose family Girolamo had chased from Forlì when he took power, had a message sent to Caterina by an arrow shot over the walls of Ravaldino, suggesting that she and he marry. As the boy was young and handsome, he would soon gain access to her, although not to her heritage. But for the moment, 12,000 Milanese soldiers neared Ravaldino, prepared for battle and for the inevitable sacking of Forlì, their reward. Learning that they were approaching, the Orsi brothers hurried to put their threat into action before being forced to flee: as a lesson for those who would defy them in the future, they went to kill Caterina's children. Happily, they had been hidden away by Bishop Savelli, whose presence had truly been a godsend. The Forlivesi themselves had a sudden change of heart. They now cried out "Ottaviano!," the name of Girolamo's heir, the boy who had nearly had his throat slit. The lad, under the protection of Savelli, was brought to them, totally mystified by the events that he had in no way been responsible for, and was paraded around the main square of the city three times, symbolizing that he was now accepted as the new lord of Forlì.

When Caterina had regained control, she coolly dismissed the thousands of soldiers who had come to her recue and were waiting to enter and ransack the city. Soldiers always earned part of their pay thusly, an accepted practice recognized by everyone. But Caterina told them, with mind-boggling dispassion and courage, that as the Forlì had stolen everything she possessed, what the soldiers would take in sacking the city belonged, in reality, to her. More incredible still, the soldiers let her get away with it. As for the Orsi, they left Forlì in search of asylum elsewhere and historically simply vanished from the face of the earth. They did leave their father behind, however, who, at age eighty, was dragged from his bed cursing his sons *for not having succeeded*! His palace was torn down and the old man pulled through the streets tied upside down to the back of a horse, his head smashed to a pulp against the cobblestones.

In neighboring Faenza its ruler Galeotto Manfredi was murdered by his wife. Just being married and having children was normally sufficient for a woman during the Renaissance; a wife's husband's extramarital indiscretions were his business. Women were watched over and chastity belts really existed to keep women from unlawful intercourse and from pleasuring themselves, the absence of which made them more desiring of their husband's attentions. But Francesca Bentivoglio, Galeotto's wife, was an exceptional woman whose father just happened to be the ruler of Bologna. Her rival was a beauty known as the Peacock, whom Galeotto was rumored to have secretly married before meeting Francesca, making him a bigamist. Francesca's father knew about the affair and tried to get his son-in-law to mend his ways but failed. When Francesca discovered the truth, she hastily returned home, certain that Galeotto would poison her. Through the good offices of Lorenzo *Il Magnifico* she returned to Galeotto, but only to have him assassinated. The murder was slapsticks comedy, with three assassins hiding under the bed and one behind the bedroom door. In the ensuing struggle it was purportedly Francesca who delivered the decisive blow, a dagger plunged into her husband's chest. But before dying Galeotto had done at least one thing right, he had fathered Astorre Manfredi, the most beautiful boy in Renaissance Italy.

With the death of Galeotto, Milan decided that Faenza would be a small although valuable gem to add to Milan's possessions. But Lorenzo *Il Magnifico*, although an ally of Milan, didn't want the Milanese to extend their control so far to the south. Lorenzo lacked troops but not intelligence. He spread rumors that Faenza would soon be sacked by the troops outside of Forlì, the troops that Caterina had prevented from entering her town. Their descent on Faenza was imminent, said Lorenzo, rousing the inhabitants into action. The outcome was chaos that Pope Innocent VIII ended by issuing an edict, in 1488, confirming three-year-old Astorre Manfredi as lord of Faenza and named an eight-member regency of noble citizens to care for the lad and the city-state. The boy had now embarked on the world stage. His mother, Francesca the assassin, remained safely in Bologna. At the same time that little Astorre was made prince of Faenza, Caterina's child Ottaviano was confirmed as ruler of Imola and Forlì, under the regency of Caterina.

Humanism played a great part in the education of the young Astorre. It consisted of classical authors, especially Cicero, and included studies in philosophy, history, rhetoric, grammar, mathematics, poetry, music and astronomy. Based on the Greek ideal of a sound mind in a sound body, it included also archery, dance and swimming. There was hunting, which boys took to naturally. Humanists insisted on the genius of man, on morality and on the extraordinary potential of the human mind. Schooling was for rich boys but places were available for poor students of recognized ability. A model education combined the classics with the basics of Christianity. Once a boy developed himself intellectually and physically, he was in the ideal position to become an ideal man, as well as having prepared himself for the best possible afterlife. Latin as well as Tuscan vernacular were in usage. Dante wrote his works in Tuscan Italian, as did the wonderful Boccaccio. One of Caterina's lovers, Pietro Bembo, helped establish Tuscan Italian as the language of the entire peninsula. Bembo later warmed Lucrezia Borgia's bed.

Erasmus was named the Prince of Humanists. Before the arrival of humanism men believed in eternal salvation after death, but philosophers such as Erasmus preached the enrichment of life in the here and now. According to him, the church had to free itself of superstitious and corrupt behavior. It had to drop its pomp, relics and beads used as magical charms. Cults based on saints and indulgences, the purpose of which was to make money by reducing the time believers would spend in hell, had to be proscribed. (One priest was fond of telling people that as soon as a coin rings in his proffered bowl, the soul for whom it is paid will fly out of purgatory and wing straight to heaven.) He fiercely believed in free will, without which human moral action would have no meaning. He accused monks, priests and popes of living in luxury after taking vows of poverty, of caring for their own needs before those of their flocks. Life began in the womb, he wrote, and one shouldn't be baptized until old enough to accept Christ. He believed that lust was a natural body function like the need to eat. He denounced those who waged war as beasts and he pitied the stupidity, ignorance and gullibility of the "faithful". Erasmus favored circumcision (although he would have been better off letting boys decide for themselves, after puberty, as he did for baptisms). He is idealized by gay groups for being homosexual, while heterosexuals furiously deny it.

Thanks to the Gutenberg Press, Erasmus's books were known far and wide. Nearly 4,000 pages could be produced by movable type per week compared to several pages that were hand copied. Erasmus could thusly publish thousands of copies of his books, making him a best seller (750,000 of his works were sold during his lifetime alone). The advance in mass publication was due to three factors: the use of the screw press, known since antiquity and used for crushing grapes and olives; the invention of metal type, in this case finding a perfect alloy consisting of lead, tin and antimony (which gives type its hardness); and the proper ink, which was oil based, more durable than water based. Gutenberg's press played a key role in the dissemination of knowledge to the masses, breaking forever the monopoly of literacy held by the nobles. By year 1500 there were 77 cities throughout Italy that had printing shops.

Erasmus formed a long friendship with Thomas More, a supposed humanist whose reputation was considerably muddied by the six executions for heresy he ordered during his chancellorship. Thomas More was against the Reformation, which cost him his life under Henry VIII, who himself died in his bed in terrible pain, small retribution for the thousands of woman, boys and men he'd had hanged or beheaded for one reason or another.

The time had come for Lucrezia to marry again, a marriage which would, naturally, benefit the pope. Alexander thusly chose the son of Duke Ercole of Ferrara, another Alfonso, Alfonso d'Este, for his daughter Lucrezia. Behind closed doors the Duke of Ferrara laughed at such pretention. His family was noble, old and wealthy, that of Alexander hick parvenus. Ercole had heard stories about them all, that Alexander had prostitutes from the best bordellos brought to him after dinner, that Cesare slept during the day and whored at night, that both he and his dad had shared Lucrezia, that they were murderous slime, socially nonexistent and morally rotten to the core.

Yet ... his own boy was perhaps little better. Alfonso was known to have two interests in life, making cannons in his own personal foundry and parading around town at night, his sword in one hand, his erect cock in the other. His former wife had been so fed up with him that she turned to women for satisfaction. Stories of incest, sodomy, rape, murder, *et j'en passe* may seem exaggerated, but personally I believe they represent just the tip of the iceberg. The repressive atmosphere during the deep darkness that followed the fall of Imperial Rome was such that when the light finally came, when the period known as the Renaissance finally rose from ancient Rome's ashes, the liberation--intellectual, artistic and sexual--was such that Italy knew few bounds. And this liberation came to a people that just happened to be among the most beautiful created by the fertile mind of God.

Ferrara Castle

But the wedding did take place since Louis XII of France wanted it, all because he needed the Borgias to further his ambitions. The price Ercoli demanded would have been dismissed out of hand by any other person in Italy, but not Alexander who disposed of literally bottomless resources, resources brought in, in multiple ways, every single day, via every church in the Christian world. Alfonse was 26, Lucrezia still only 21. Parties were thrown in Rome prior to Lucrezia leaving the city, one of which, in 1501, was the famous Banquet of the Chestnuts, during which prizes were given to those who could ejaculate the most times and copulate with the most prostitutes. Some say Lucrezia was present. Some put Cesare there. Others place them both. All named Alexander (see Chapter Thirteen).

Later Sancia would visit her dear friend Lucrezia becoming, during her stay, the mistress of Lucrezia's husband Alfonso.

The trip to Ferrara and the celebration there cost a fortune, but the wedding night came off well. Alexander was told that Alfonso had contented Lucrezia that night and then took his pleasure with other women during the day. The pope supposedly thought this just fine as Alfonso was a young man and, as such, multiple adventures were good for him. The historian Johann Burchard wrote that all the talk of lubricity inspired the pope to increase the number of prostitutes he welcomed into his rooms that night. As always in Italy, love was in the air.

In Forlì love was also in the air. Caterina decided to see Antonio Maria Ordelaffi, he who had sent her a billet-doux by arrow when she was holed up in Ravaldino. Their relationship lasted months, during which the Forlivesi happily anticipated the coming marriage. After all, Caterina, decided and intelligent as she was, was nonetheless a woman and as such needed male direction. (No matter what she accomplished, the idea that she depended on men would hold true until her death.) But Caterina had other ideas. She had had her eye on a stable boy, Giacomo Feo, since he was fifteen. Now seventeen, tall, lithe and supranormally handsome, his contemporaries tell us he was big where it counted. When Caterina found herself pregnant, she secretly married the kid.

All hell broke out in every direction. Forlivesi and Imolesi couldn't accept the primacy of a stable boy over their cities, and Bologna, Milan, Florence and Ferrara proclaimed that they had youths of noble birth who could satisfy the countess at least as well as Feo. The city that eventually won out, should Caterina choose one of their boys, would not only broaden its territory thanks to its influence over the two city-states, but it would control a major artery through the Apennines. Foiled attempts were made on the lives of both the countess and her lad, but she brought her pregnancy to term, giving birth to a baby boy,

Bernardino. The marriage and the baby were kept secret because she did not want to undermine the ascension of Girolamo's son Ottaviano. She thusly decided to end any rumors concerning one or the other by punishing the rumormongers. She had them systematically beaten, many of whom were permanently maimed and at least one was killed. But it was a wonderful period for Caterina. A visiting ambassador was allowed into the inner sanctum of Caterina's palace where she and Giacomo were playing with Catherina's children by Girolamo and her son by Feo. He described the husband and wife, in the light of the setting sun, as pure angels.

In 1492 two major events occurred. Lorenzo *Il Magnifico* died, bringing an end to the golden age of the Italian Renaissance, and Rodrigo Borgia became Pope Alexander VI, the warrior pope who would, in his way, also aid in the demise of the Renaissance. Lorenzo: absolute good--in the context of the Renaissance; Alexander VI: absolute bad--even for the Renaissance. His chances at being elected had been small as he and Jorge da Costa of Portugal were the only non-Italians out of 23 cardinals.

Naturally, 1492 was also known for Columbus's discovery of the Americas and the year Magellan germinated the idea of circumnavigating the world.

Giacomo Feo, the stable boy, now decided politics for the two city-states, certain that he knew as much or more than seasoned kings, counts, ambassadors and other diplomats. So when Ottaviano, now a man at age 16, went to his mother and demanded that he be recognized as the new count of Forlì and Imola, an argument ensued that ended with Feo slapping the boy, who stormed out of the room red-faced. A week later, as Feo was riding through the woods along with Caterina, a group of friends approached them on horse. As Feo chatted amiably with one, another stuck a dagger in his back. Caterina had the presence of mind to turn and ride off to the impregnable shelter of Ravaldino. Feo's bodyguards also took flight, leaving the handsome boy to fall from his horse into a ditch.

The people of Forlì remembered the heads Caterina ordered cut off after the assassination of Girolama and her victory from the crenelated summits of Ravaldino. So when the murderers of Feo came riding into the town square, their clothes filthy with his blood, shouting to all the account of their exploits which, they maintained, were designed to give power over Forlì and Imola to their rightful count, Ottaviano, a group of nobles thought best to go to Ravaldino to find out what Caterina thought of it all. When they returned, they ordered the arrest of the assassins. The reprisals were indeed terrible. The murderers had their heads axed open, from the top to the chin. Their wives and mistresses and children were slaughtered. Their houses were torn down brick by brick. Two babies associated with them, age three and nine months, along with their nurses, were bludgeoned to death. An accused priest was dragged behind a horse, his head fractured against the cobblestones, as Caterina had ordered done to Girolamo's assassin, old man Orsi. Under torture another conspirator gave out the name of her son Ottaviano, known by all to have hated Feo for usurping his rightful place as count of Forlì and Imola. Caterina had her son arrested, an act so horrifying that the inhabitants followed the boy to the gates of Ravaldino where Caterina dispersed them with cannon fire. After a stormy meeting with his mother, the boy was put under house arrest. At Feo's funeral all of Forlì and Imola turned out, so afraid were the populations of their countess. Heaven entered the act by bringing down a plague on the people: rashes appeared on their genitals and their lymph nodes swelled up. The syphilis epidemic had begun. Caterina ordered her palace torn down because it had sheltered both her and Feo, and his statue in bronze was raised in his honor. A new palace was built on the grounds of fortified Ravaldino, its furnishings and gardens so exquisite that Caterina called it Paradise. She sent Ottaviano to Florence to learn the art of war. The sixteen-year-old lad, a veritable Don Juan like his father Girolamo, left behind mistresses and bastards.

Ravaldino, Caterina's Paradise.

Around this time Caterina is thought to have tried to kill Alexander himself by sending the pope a gift wrapped either in poison designed to work by absorption through the skin or through inhalation, or wrapped in tissue imbibed in the sweat of plague victims, perhaps the first historical example of germ warfare, a tale historically so persistent that it may really have taken place.

Caterina had eight children. Bianca Riario was her only girl and Caterina destined her for the handsome Astorre Manfredi of neighboring Faenza. All the surrounding powers had their say in the matter, some for and some against, but the negatives and positives equaled themselves out. For Caterina the union of the lad, age ten, and the lass, age fourteen, would unify the region, as Faenza was exactly in the middle between Forlì and Imola. Faenza was ruled by a Council which was doing an excellent job of both educating the young Astorre and of governing the tiny city-state. A pretender, however, Ottaviano Manfredi, Astorre's cousin, decided that the time was perfect for him to take power from the boy who was still a child. The resulting disorder attracted the attention of Venice who was always on the lookout for an easy kill. Bologna came to the same conclusion, as did Milan. The brouhaha dissuaded Caterina from pursuing the marriage with Astorre and it was therefore annulled. Bianca would finally find a suitor, a count from the region of Parma, when she attained the ripe old age of twenty-two.

For Caterina, marital bliss occurred much sooner. At age thirty-three she fell in love with Giovanni de' Medici, thirty, perhaps the first veritably educated man in her life, who was also handsome and charming. They were secretly married because of Ludovico of Milan's enmity towards Florence. Knowing that he would find out anyway, Caterina tried to soothe Ludovico's anger by naming her only child with Giovanni after him, Ludovico Sforza de' Medici. Incredibly, her new husband Giovanni had inherited, in spades, the ills of his ancestors: he died in Caterina's arms, probably of complications due to family gout. In his memory she renamed her child Giovanni Sforza de' Medici.

That Caterina's private life was in shambles didn't mean she couldn't try to find happiness for her children. So when Alexander VI, her son Ottaviano's godfather, suggested a marriage between the boy and Lucrezia, Alexander's daughter, she knew that this would be the first step in turning over Forlì and Imola to the pope. Such a marriage could also turn out to be disastrous for her boy, Ottaviano. Caterina remembered that Lucrezia's first husband had been declared impotent after three years of marriage despite the boy's outcry that he'd had her "at least a thousand times". In order to protect her boy Caterina refused Alexander's offer, and in the nick of time too. The next candidate, Alfonso, was strangled on Cesare's orders.

Alexander decided on the direct approach and sent Cesare to bring Forlì and Imola into the lap of the Papal States. Caterina put the finishing touches on the defenses of Ravaldino just as Cesare arrived at the head of an army of twelve thousand of Louis XII's French troops. After promising her money and a palace of her own in Rome, the tone between the two--Cesare on his white charger facing the closed drawbridge to Ravaldino, Caterine atop the crenellated tower--turned sour as one insulted the other. They split up but after a few hours of reflection Cesare returned. This time Caterina was standing on the lowered drawbridge. Cesare dismounted and approached the edge. Luckily for him, he was in beauty that day. The terrible traces of his syphilis had temporarily disappeared. Handsome and gorgeously dressed in black velvet, a rarity during the period when both sexes preferred bright colors (after the austerity of the Middle Ages), he decided to trade the filthy language he was partial to with the troops, for the sparkling oratory of the likes of Cicero. Caterina too was in beauty, her breasts propped up by a tight bodice. She was immediately aware that Cesare had come to seduce her with a stunning smile similar to that used by Stanley Kowalski to mollify his wife Stella. Caterina, with the same intention, turned a welcoming shoulder in his direction, he held out a hand to touch it, she enticingly took a step back in the direction of the door to Ravaldino, he followed ... until he felt the drawbridge rising under his feet. He jumped off just in time to see Caterina disappear behind the closing rampart. Cesare, his face red with shame for having been tricked, stormed off.

Sadly, Cesare would win out. What Caterina had pointed to when the Orsi had put a dagger against the throat of her son when ordering her to surrender Ravaldino, what one contemporary had referred to as her "cunt" in a letter to Lorenzo *Il Magnifico*, would soon be not only his, but his until he himself felt that his humiliation of her had gone on long enough. (Although some writers during the period suggested that she grew to *like* Cesare and his form of humiliation which, naturally, we'll never ever know.)

At any rate, Cesare immediately went back to his obscene military language and ordered an all-out attack on the citadel. I won't go into the actual destruction except to say that she was betrayed from inside the walls, walls opened to Cesare and his French troops. The Italians inside were spared but ransomed; the mercenaries under Caterina had their throats slit. She stepped over seven hundred strewn corpses on her way out of Ravaldino, in time to see her monument of bronze to her beloved Feo being carted away prior to being melted into cannon balls. Feo was symptomatic of what had undermined her place in Forlì and Imola: she had fought for her own pleasure and a place in the sun for her children; she had known hundreds of lads and wealth and luxury beyond measure; and so as one citizen summed it all up as she was hauled away, "She had put her faith in herself and in the walls of her fortress, and none in the people she ruled".

The French commanders observed the fate of the women left behind, their thighs spread as the men lined up. They knew that the prettiest had already been set aside for themselves later on. Realizing what was in store for Caterina, several tried to save the countess by telling Cesare that they had precedence over her and would assure her safety right up to the moment she came before King Louis XII. This hiatus ended in an exchange of money. Cesare retired with the countess while the French officers, rich, sought the comfort of the naked forms awaiting them under the covers of their own beds. One of them was heard to say, as he unbuttoned his superb military tunic, ''Well, at least she won't be wanting for fucking.''

CHAPTER EIGHT

ASTORRE MANFREDI MURDERED IN ROME
CATERINA SFORZA DIES IN FLORENCE
Faenza, Francesca Bentivoglio, Astorre Manfredi, Gianevangelista Manfredi, Caterina Riario Sforza de' Medici, Giovanni de' Medici, Giovanni dalle Bande Nere, Siena, Bernard Stewart d'Aubigny, Machiavelli

After the fall of Imola and Forlì Cesare was welcome back in Rome in a frenzy of excitement. His father Pope Alexander ordered all the clergy, all the cardinals, all officials and ambassadors to turn out to cheer his entry into the Eternal City, along with Romans who lined the streets as he passed, trumpets blaring, Cesare and his entourage of hundreds dressed in Cesarean black, others in the new attire he had adopted, the red and gold of France. He kissed his father on the feet, the hands and the mouth. Banners were raised above the Castel Sant'Angelo where he would live, and from its towers cannons fired hundreds of rounds. Rarely had the gods raised so high someone they were prepared to bring so low. He was protected by his troops, led by the likes of the Orsini, the Bentivoglii, the Baglioni, Pandolfo Petrucci, the Vitelli, Oliverotto and others, all of whom would soon betray their glorious leader.

As with all seventeen-year-olds, Astorre Manfredi had everything to live for. Of medium height, with a boyish chest and slim waist, his eyes were blue and his hair as blond as gold--curly waves of which descended to his shoulders. He was courteous, had a good word for everyone, and was as aware of his charm and sexual appeal as is every Italian boy, then as today. His family had ruled the city-state of Faenza for two centuries, and although there had been some bad apples, the Manfredi, in general, had done somewhat better than the other lords, dukes and princes of the Romagna. Astorre himself was loved. Although the real power behind Faenza lay with the Council that had been regent since Astorre Manfredi was named lord at age three, he had his word to say and that word was listened to more and more frequently. Faenza was one of the few veritable free spirits to exist outside Florence, and it was more of a Republic than even the Florentine city.

Indeed, Astorre had everything to live for, and perhaps even a bit more as he had received the best education available. Private tutors had instructed him in Latin, even if his daily speech was in the Italian vernacular. He had read Homer and Plato, the Greek tragedians, Suetonius and Xenophon and Plutarch, he had studied the texts of Cicero and was himself on the road to becoming an accomplished speaker.

Although puberty came later than it does today, he had already known girls and women. In fact, his extreme beauty brought blushes to the maidens in the market. His marriage to Caterina's daughter Bianca had fallen through but it was of little consequence as there were plenty of other matches to be made with girls from far more important towns than were Forlì and Imola.

Faenza was well fortified, but its strategic location meant it was in continual danger from this power or that. Like the deterrent the atomic bomb offers today, Faenza, being surrounded by powers such as Bologna, Milan, Florence and Venice, was protected because if one power dared attack, the others would tear it to pieces in order to maintain the status quo. Faenza was fortified, but with Cesare prowling around the region the citizens of the city-state decided to add to their battlements and ensure that neighboring cities would come to their succor if and when needed.

Astorre's first appeal for support went to neighboring Bologna. After all, his mother was the sister of Giovanni Bentivoglio, the lord of Bologna. Bentivoglio sent a thousand troops to Faenza but was later forced to withdraw them due to pressure from both the French King Louis XII and the pope who threatened excommunication. Louis thanked Bentivoglio for the withdrawal by taking Bologna under his wing, thus preserving the city from future ravages by Cesare. The pope also sent a note of thanks. As a sign of further capitulation, Bentivoglio agreed to feed and house a large number of Louis and Cesare's soldiers. Astorre appealed to Venice, a power he could usually depend upon, but Venice too was afraid of Louis and besides, when Louis overran Milan he had adroitly given certain lands adjoining Venice to the Serenissima, that was now in his debt.

When Cesare did more than prowl, when he attacked and ravaged neighboring Forlì and Imola, Faenzans were armed and readied for action. At first Cesare tried charm. He met with the Council and with Astorre, informing them that the time had come for Faenza--like Forlì and Imola--to return to the lap of the Papal States under the direction of their pope, Alexander VI. Nothing would change other than papal troops being stationed in the fort, in addition to Faenzans being enrolled in the ever-more-numerous papal armies. Astorre and the Council didn't accept Cesare's offer, as he probably knew they wouldn't, but it gave Cesare a chance to judge them both. He loved the boy as did the Faenzans, and he was known to bed lads that caught his fancy, a bent that amused his men, many of whom shared the same drift. An educated beauty would be a change from his usual bronzed and husky country fare.

Cesare had far bigger fish in mind than tiny Faenza but he couldn't just bypass it. It was at the entrance to the Apennines and it controlled an important route, the Via Emilia. Anyway, if he let a little fish get away, just because he liked the ruling prince, what chance would he have with bigger states? So he attacked. To his immense surprise the Faenzans defended themselves tooth and nail, even the women took up arms. Priests melted down sacred objects to provide money. The wealthy gave up their stocks of wheat and wine. The siege went on and on until the coming of winter, the winter of 1500, more than normally cold and snowy. Leaving enough men to make certain that Faenza wasn't supplied in food and weapons, Cesare went to spend winter in Cesena, a locality he liked so much he was thinking of making it, when all power was in his hands, the capital of the Romagna. He spent money like water, offering games, tournaments and processions, and organized huge festivities at Christmas and during Carnival. He showed his prowess by challenging the local boys to wrestling matches and horse races, all of which made him immensely popular. His admiration for the people of Faenza was such that when a merchant escaped Faenza and came to Cesena with important information concerning which parts of the walls were the less secure, Cesare had the man publicly hanged.

With the coming of spring, in March to be exact, Cesare returned to Faenza where he bombarded the walls of the city for five months, concentrating on the spot revealed by the Faenzan traitor. As food and water were lacking and the dead were piling up, as there were fewer stones and hot pitch to cast down on the invaders, Astorre and the Council were obliged to seek a truce. Cesare had no reason to give the Faenzans anything. Victory was his. But he did like the lad, and it had always been his policy to be as lenient as possible with a population. In that way he could count on the defeated to provide him with food once they had returned to the fields, as well as to give shelter for his men and horses and furnish the cannon fodder--their sons--necessary to win battles. In addition, the Council paid him personally 40,000 ducats. So, good-humoredly, he offered the boy what he wanted, and the boy wanted everything. He wanted Faenza free of foreign troops, he wanted Faenzans to be able to keep their possessions, and he wanted Cesare to forbid sacking and rape. All Astorre had to do in exchange was sign over the town to Alexander VI, which he and the Council agreed to do.

Astorre and his fifteen-year-old half-brother Gianevangelista were given their freedom, but to Cesare's astonishment they wanted to accompany him to Rome, as today kids want to see the lights of New York. Both boys also deeply admired the most virile, courageous and experienced warrior in recent Italian history. To learn from him would make them men on the way up; Cesare was their elevator to the very top floor. It was a fatal mistake because bright lights rarely come without the accompanying greed, vice and corruption that carpet the walls in shadows.

In 1502 Astorre Manfredi's naked body came to the surface of the Tiber, caught in a fisherman's net, attached to that of his brother. Johann Burchard wrote that both boys had been participants in an orgy along with a large number of very young girls. Whether they freely consented to take part or were forced, will never be known. Whether the orgy even took place, will never be known. Cesare was said to have been involved--it would have been far from his first bacchanalia. Perhaps his father took part too. Burchard only says that "a certain powerful person sated his lust" on the boy. Machiavelli gets into the act because he had been there to give Cesare advice, one piece of which we find in his book: "When a prince assumes power over a conquered territory his first obligation, if he wishes to preserve that power, is to destroy the rulers in place." Every time, in Italian politics, that this principle hadn't been observed, the prince lived to regret it. Turks systematically had their brothers garroted as their very first act on ascending to the throne. It's true that had Astorre lived he might have eventually become a problem for Cesare. Already immensely popular in his hometown, Astorre might have outshone Cesare himself in public adulation, an intolerable risk to a man who wore impeccable black velvet and paraded around on a white charger adorned with bells, his stirrups made of silver, his spurs of gold, but a man who was aging, a man with "flowers".

Burchard says that Astorre and his brother Gianevangelista had been attached together with a stone tied to their necks. Females, all naked, had been tied together in the same fashion. The boys' bodies had torture marks.

Cesare pushed his fiendishness to extremes by greeting an envoy from Venice and springing on him the news of the murders, knowing that Venice had taken a special and highly favorable interest in both Faenza and Astorre Manfredi. The envoy was said to have not even blinked, unsurprising for a city where slaves could still be purchased, their prices varying from six ducats for a man to a hundred for a beddable girl. Burchard ends his story of Astorre by saying that, "The young man was of such unequaled beauty and intelligence that it would be impossible to find another as sterling as he in all of Italy." The boy was 17. The year was 1502.

As for Caterina, she had been taken to the Castel Sant'Angelo, over which she had once reigned. She was said to have deeply regretted those she had murdered after the assassinations of Girolamo and Feo, a score for the first, two score for the second. Life supposedly meant little at the time, yet I remain convinced that individuals during the Renaissance wanted to live out their lives, just as we do today, to the last moment. They certainly were barbarous, hanging people until they were nearly dead, then cutting them down, still alive, so they could watch themselves be disemboweled or have their hearts cut out still beating, or, the horror of horrors, have their privates cut away and stuffed in their mouths to suffocate on. The rape of women was an essential perk of war, as was ransacking and destruction. Children died unnecessarily, some before the eyes of their parents. So Caterina had reason to repent and beg for God's forgiveness. We certainly have reason to be thankful for our own more civilized times ... if, naturally, one excludes the Great War responsible for 20,000,000 deaths, the Second that caused twice that, and, more recently, the slaughter of 8,000 boys age 13 and over in Srebrenica, all of whom certainly begged for their precious lives right up to the last horrifying second.

Caterina was taken to Castel Sant'Angelo and locked away out of the reach of those like Cesare and his close friends who would be able to crow over having possessed the charms of the Cleopatra who hadn't gotten away. Her pain deepened when she discovered that her sons, Ottaviano and Cesare, were doing just fine under the rule of Alexander, from whom both boys sought the red hat of a cardinal. With mistresses and bastards galore, they were certainly on the right path to seeing their wishes fulfilled. News from Florence informed her that her last husband's brother was dilapidating the fortune Giovanni de' Medici had willed to her and his son, little Giovanni.

At age ten Caterina had visited Florence with her father Galeazzo Maria Sforza and had been welcomed by Lorenze *Il Magnifico* himself. Thanks to the intervention of Louis XII, who respected her as a ruler and as a warrior, she was freed from Castel Sant'Angelo--after signing over Forlì and Imola to Alexander. She made her way back to Florence, the most beautiful and cultivated city of the Renaissance, where she would die. In an ending that was almost a fairytale of beauty, she was met there by her sons Ottaviano, Cesare, Galeazzo, Sforzino, and Bernardino--the son of Feo. Her only daughter, the loyal Bianca, was also waiting for her, holding in her arms little Giovanni, the son of her last love, Giovanni de' Medici, whose fortune his brother had not entirely dilapidated--in fact, there remained enough so that Caterina could live in comfort and offer sums to her sons who never ever stopped making requests for this and that, just as they had, when infants, lustily and greedily suckled at the breasts of their wet nurses.

To save her soul she made donations to convents and churches, especially to the convent of Muratte where she asked to be interred. These donations were to Christ, for it is to Christ that women turn when they are no longer of an age to welcome virile lovers. She passed away at age forty-six. The year was 1509. Her tomb was desecrated 300 years later and her remains lost when Muratte became a prison (8).

But before we part company with this truly remarkable woman, perhaps a word about her last son, little Giovanni, son of Giovanni de' Medici. Different from the other Medici, he spurned intellectual activities in favor of martial interests. He often ran away from home and liked the company of simple farm boys. At age twelve he killed one and at age thirteen he raped a boy of sixteen. Trying desperately to save him, Florentine nobles put him under the control of an ambassador, Salviati, who was named to Rome. There Giovanni slummed with lowlifes, in perpetual trouble. He became a condottiere and was known for exclaiming, ''I rule with my ass in the saddle and a sword in my fist!'' Pope

Leo X chose him to police Rome, and then to form an army using men of normally irredeemable depravity that only Giovanni had the force to make into manageable soldiers. He specialized in lightning strikes with a preference for ambushes. His motto was, "I embrace my rivals in order to strangle them." When his patron Pope Leo X died, Giovanni added black stripes to his armor, for which he is known historically as Giovanni dalle Bande Nere. He married Salviati's daughter and had a son destined to become lord of Florence. Severely wounded in battle, he had to have his foot amputated, ten men needed to hold him down. He died five days later of gangrene. He was the very last of the condottieri. Of his direct descendants, other than fathering a Florentine lord, one, Marie de' Medici, became Queen of France--but led a terribly sorrowful life (7). (The Florentine lord he sired was Cosimo I who would rule Florence, employ Michelangelo, and encourage Cellini to give birth to a miracle equal to Michelangelo's *David*, Cellini's *Perseus* [5].)

For Cesare, Caterina, Forlì and Imola were an interlude to much bigger acts of bravura. He went on to take Urbino, the citadel of the Montefeltro, and a dozen other city-states. Along the way he heard stories about some of his captains, traitors in the pay of Roman nobles eager for the reign of Alexander to come to an end by assassinating their leader, Cesare.

He moved on to Siena, sacking, destroying, maiming, killing and raping. Those who wouldn't surrender their money were tortured; if they were found to have nothing to give up, their throats were slashed (the soldiers were instructed that this was the best way not to blunt a sharp sword or dagger).

The French army of 14,000, accompanied by Cesare and led by Bernard Stewart d'Aubigny, a Scotsman by birth, made its way to Naples, accompanied by, Burchard tells us, a very inadequate number of prostitutes: 16. On the way only Capua put up a fight, but the town was betrayed from someone inside. This person, as well as the entire population, women, children, priests and nuns, were slaughtered as a warning to the towns to come, slaughtered after serving the men's sexual needs. When the troops entered Naples, there was no confrontation. Cesare was rewarded with 40,000 ducats. He was 26.

As for d'Aubigny, he returned to England where he headed the army that placed Henry Tudor on the throne, the man crowned as Henry VII. In the Introduction I mentioned certain incredible events taking place at the time that kept Europe's kings and queens on the edge of their thrones. The story of Henry VII and Perkin is one such event, covered in Chapter Twelve.

A new Venetian ambassador was sent to the Vatican, Antonio Giustinian, a man of great importance to us because we are informed about much that follows thanks to the hundreds of letters he wrote and sent throughout Europe. Around this time too Florence sent a delegation to Cesare Borgia who had just taken Urbino, in order to both calm the young man's ardors for conquest and to get his support in maintaining Florence's authority over Pisa and Arezzo. The delegation consisted of Francesco Soderini, the brother of the courant head of Florence, and a new man destined to leave his mark on the world, Niccolò Machiavelli. Niccolò Machiavelli served Cesare Borgia, which allowed him an eyewitness-view of ruthless government, the basis of his masterpiece *The Prince*, the very foundation of today's political science. We don't know to what extent Machiavelli carried on male-male relations during his adult life, but thanks to Michael Rocke and his wonderful book *Forbidden Friendships* we have this response from Machiavelli to the letter sent to him by a childhood friend who is worried about his son's frequentations, proof of Machiavelli's appreciation of boys during his own adolescence: "Since we are verging on old age, we might be severe and overly scrupulous, and we do not remember what we did as adolescents. So Lodovico has a boy with him, with whom he amuses himself, jests, takes walks, growls in his ear, goes to bed together. What then? Even in these things perhaps there is nothing bad." (*Growls* in his ear: I *adore* that!)

Machiavelli is also said to have exclaimed: "In your house there are no young boys and women to fuck. What kind of a fucking house is that?"

Machiavelli.
About Cesare Borgia Machiavelli wrote: 'He was the handsomest man of his times.'

Few other times in history were more tumultuous than those known to Machiavelli. Just the mention of names such as the Visconti, the Sforza, the Borgia, Charles VIII, the warrior pope Julius II, the Turks brought instant fear to the hearts of men. Battles between the city-states continued without ever a respite. Quarrels between the Medici and their fellow citizens led to the assassination of Lorenzo's brother Giuliano by the Pazzi. Religious unrest caused by the likes of Savonarola, and the decadence of Pope Alexander VI, provoked riots and turmoil. Privileged youths such as Cesare and his brothers--and nearly every other boy-delinquent of noble blood--were free to kill, maim and rape. Condottieri were encouraged to recuperate their wages by destroying villages, towns and cities, and to assuage their lust on captured girls and women. To these inflictions can be added disease and plague--so terrible that noble families farmed out their children until around age seven, the age at which they were allowed to return home had they survived the various ailments of the times. Even the peaceable Machiavelli--for reasons unknown to us--was tortured by the usually civilized Medici--with the *strappado*, a torture in five degrees. In the first the prisoner's hands were tired behind his back and he was advised to confess. If he refused, his arms were raised behind his back by a rope attached to a pulley. During this second degree he was lifted off his feet for a short time. If he still refused to confess he faced the third degree, being raised until his arms dislocated. During the fourth degree he was violently jerked. During the last degree, weights were added, until his arms were torn from his body. Machiavelli went as far as the first degree, but as his purported crimes were apparently few, he was let off. He then retired from politics. In a letter to a friend he described a typical day of retirement as one in which he entered his study wearing the formal dress of an ambassador, and there he discoursed with the popes, princes, kings and emperors of old, asking them questions and noting down their answers.

CHAPTER NINE

THE REVOLT OF THE CONDOTTIERI
Vitellozzo Vitelli, Paolo Vitelli, Oliverotto of Fermo, Magione Orsini, Paolo Orsini, Roberto Orsini, Francesco Gaimbattista Orsini, Ermes Bentivolglio, Pandolfo Petrucci, Alexander VI, Ramiro de Lorca, Micheletto de Corella

Machiavelli was smitten by Cesare who became his model as the perfect condottiere. He wrote that the man never rested, thanks to which his rapid displacements took an adversary by surprise. Cesare would often summon him in the middle of the night or early morning, his syphilitic face covered in gauze.

The copyright for the scene of the mafia meeting that ends in everyone sitting around a banquet table, offered rich gifts to ease them into a spirit of tranquility and insouciance, prior to their being slaughtered, goes to Cesare Borgia and dates from 1503. Cesare surrounded himself with some of Italy's greatest tyrants and cutthroats. There was Vitellozzo Vitelli, lord of several minor towns, but known as a condottiere at the head of his own army that he placed under the highest bidder. He and his brother Paolo had fought for Florence until Paolo was put to death for supposed treachery. Vitelli then fought for Cesare, a man he respected so much he conquered the town of Senigallia as a gift to the charismatic Borgia, a gift he had to relinquish to Florence, following orders from Cesare who was himself following orders from King Louis XII, under whom Cesare had placed himself. Embittered, Vitelli met with other unhappy condottieri at

Magione to plot Cesare's downfall.

Among them was Oliverotto of Fermo. As often happens, it seems, in Hollywood productions, Oliverotto had had the original idea for the mafia-massacre-banquet scenario that Cesare later stole. Oliverotto had lost his father when very young and had been raised by his uncle Giovanni. The boy decided to strike out on his own by inviting his uncle and all the powers of Fermo to a huge dinner where armed men had been hidden in strategic recesses. At his signal the diners were slaughtered. He then joined forces with Vitelli in campaigns for and then against Pisa, for and then against Florence, for and then against Cesare. Like Vitelli, he was set on following Cesare to the ends of the earth, even capturing Camerino for him. Camerino was a small fief ruled by the da Varani since 1262. The lords now were Giulio Cesare da Varano and his three sons, all of whom Oliverotto had strangled in their castle La Pergola. Pope Alexander VI then visited the town alongside his son Cesare and installed, as Duke of Camerino, his daughter Lucrezia's four-year-old son Juan, the child she had had with the servant Pedro Calderon, the boy Cesare had murdered in the Vatican as he sought shelter in the robes of Alexander, knifing him with such fury that the boy's blood splattered the pope's face. Instead of thanking Oliverotto sufficiently for Camerino, Cesare neglected him in favor of greater men, the first of which was King Louis, leaving Oliverotto stranded along the route like an abandoned dog.

The Orsini brothers were also present at Magione, Paolo, Roberto and Francesco. A fourth brother, Cardinal Giambattista Orsini, was held back in Rome, on business. It was he the supposed brains behind the plot to destroy Cesare. Louis XII had personally told Cardinal Orsini, during the king's visit to Milan, that Cesare was determined to annihilate the Orsini, which was not only true, it was set to happened in a matter of weeks. The cardinal confronted Pope Alexander with the accusation, who assured him that his son Cesare loved the Orsini even more than his own Borgia.

Pandolfo Petrucci attended the meeting at Magione. He had gained power in Siena thanks to wealth inherited from his brother and the fortune held by his father-in-law. Petrucci used his money to put his supporters in positions of power, earning enemies, among whom was his father-in-law who plotted to have him assassinated. Petrucci struck first, murdering him in 1500. Petrucci managed Siena so deftly--avoiding wars and bringing financial stability--that he won what was literally the love of the Sienese. Convinced that he would make a far more just and competent leader than Cesare, he joined the others as the head of the revolt, along with cardinal Orsini. Fearing a trap at Senigallia where Cesare would later convoke them all, he alleged other business to stay away. After the events at Senigallia he left Siena, certain he was next on the list of planned assassinations, but returned to Siena at the insistence of Louis XII who wanted war replaced by stability. Petrucci never gained real power because there was always someone still more competent or ambitious than he, Pope Julius II, for example, whom he admired. Before turning over Siena to his son, he was thought to have been behind the death of Pius III who was pope for 26 days, poisoning him in order to make way for Julius II.

The Bentivoglio family had held Bologna since the early 1300s, a town with an extremely important university that had carried out medical dissections in public for centuries. The leader now, Giovanni Bentivoglio, had done whatever he could to gain the favor of King Louis XII and Cesare, even withdrawing the troops he had promised in support of Faenza, ruled by his daughter's son, Astorre Manfredi. He surrendered fortifications to Cesare and put food and lodging at the disposition of a part of his troops. But then Louis withdrew his support, saying he couldn't stand in the way of Pope Alexander VI who had final supremacy over Bologna. Afraid that Cesare would take possession of the city, Giovanni sent his son Ermes to Magione to join the other conspirators. The young Ermes proclaimed, in front of the participants, that he himself would kill Cesare.

Gian Paolo Baglioni was also present at Magione. Lord of Perugia, he was at Oliverotto and Vitelli's sides in massacring the citizens of Camerino. He escaped Cesare's vengeance at Senigallia but was later beheaded in Rome for his role in an attempted assassination, supposedly a pretext used by the Medici pope Leo X because Baglioni was a cruel tyrant who was becoming far too strong.

The catalyst for the meeting of these gentlemen in Magione was a rumor, that King Louis XII of France feared that Alexander VI sought the union of all of Italy under his son Cesare Borgia. This meant that both Spain, which occupied Naples, and France, which occupied Milan, would be escorted *manu militari* out of the country. The rumor gave courage to those who had loyally served he who was now referred to as Valentino, Cesare's name since Louis made him Duke of Valence. The men at Magione felt that Cesare had been loyally served, and had given nothing back in exchange. Worse, he had deprived most of the men of their conquests, if in doing so he could further his own ambitions and/or ingratiate himself to the all-powerful French king. Others, like the Bentivoglii, just wanted to keep that which had been theirs for generations, more and more difficult with the fearless, pitiless and ambitious son of the pope roaming about. Some of the complotters, those who believed the rumor, even envisioned the possibility that Louis would take Cesare back to France with him and imprison him for life, as the French had done to Ludovico Sforza.

Besides the men mentioned above, there were other complotters who took a backseat, waiting to see in which direction the wind turned: Giovanni Sforza of Pesaro and Francesco Gonsaga of Mantua. They had been present in Milan when Louis rode out to personally welcome Cesare, calling him *"mon ami"* and *"mon cher cousin." They* didn't believe the rumor that Alexander would expulse the French from Italy.

Pope Alexander had been previously needed by Louis for Louis' divorce and Louis' request for a cardinal's hat for his friend and counselor George d'Amboise. Now Louis wanted Alexander to put Cesare's troops under his direction in his reconquest of Naples. He also wanted Cesare to promise to have d'Amboise replace Alexander as pope following Alexander's death. Cesare left Louis in Milan and rode off into the Papal States and the Romagna with his and Louis' combined forces, the French led by Yves d'Alègre, around 6,000 in number. Alexander prepared the way by issuing bulls excommunicating Romagna's lords for not paying sufficient obeisance to their suzerain, the pope himself.

So at Magione they all came together, even Vitelli, so stricken by syphilis that he couldn't even walk and had to be toted around on a stretcher. Had they stuck together they would easily have won. Cesare had surrendered the mass of his troops to Louis for his move against Naples, leaving him with but a handful. The complotters, on the other hand, had a combined army of 10,000. Ermes Bentivolgio, who had promised to kill Cesare with his own hands, upped the stakes by declaring that his big brother Giovanni would march on Imola, where Cesare presently resided, and destroy both him and what remained of his troops.

Yet the moment the meeting broke up, Vitelli and the Orsini sent word to Cesare that they would remain loyal to him *in perpetuum*, while Giovanni Bentivoglio contacted Cesare through his sister Lucrezia's husband Alphonso of Ferrara, pleading for negotiations.

These dealings didn't stop the Vitelli and Baglioni from trying to take back some of the territory they had surrendered to Cesare, killing Bartolomeo da Capranica while doing so, a valued Cesare captain, and attacking Micheletto de Corella who was holding Pesaro for Cesare. Micheletto was Cesare's irreplaceable Spanish assassin, he who throttled to death Lucrezia's husband and Sancia's brother after Cesare himself had failed to kill the boy. Micheletto had strangled Francesco Troche, a loyal servant who had hoped for a cardinal's hat in recompense for his loyalty, and then badmouthed both Cesare and the pope when he didn't receive one. Micheletto is suspected of killing Astorre Manfredi at the end of an orgy organized by Cesare and, according to Burchard, attended by Alexander. He strangled Giulio Cesare da Varano, as mentioned, and slit his three sons' throats. In a version of the murders, given by the author Sabatini, one of the sons was caught by Micheletto in the market place and strangled. The boy nonetheless survived and sought sanctuary in a nearby church, the priest of which turned him over to Micheletto who cut his throat. The priest was later torn to pieces by the outraged citizens.

Cesare put off meeting with his opponents until he'd had time to gather new recruits. They came in from everywhere, crowding to serve this handsome man on his white charger, dressed all in black, totally loyal to the men who did as he wished, the possessor of endless funds raked in daily from all the churches in the known world, through Alexander VI. The new recruits were augmented by Swiss and Gascon mercenaries.

Before meeting his captains at Senigallia Cesare, accompanied by the assassin Micheletto--never a good sign--had business in Rimini with a captian he had placed over the town. Complaints reached Cesare's ears that Ramiro de Lorca was murdering whomever he wished, stealing from the inhabitants and taking any girl who caught his fancy. Cesare had already received reports of Lorcas's lascivious behavior towards Lucrezia when he'd accompanied her to her wedding with Alfonso of Ferrara. Micheletto strangled him with a violin cord.

Cesare rode to Senigallia. Not all of the traitors would be able to make it and those who did came with their own troops. As their leader, Cesare told them that his soldiers had priority in lodging. Troops other than his own were to evacuate Senigallia and find quarters outside the town limits. These Cesare had quietly surrounded by his men.

The leaders entered the castle of Senigallia where a banquet in Cesare's honor was spread out. At a certain moment Cesare excused himself to answer a call of nature. Those present, Vitelli and the Orsini brothers, Francesco and Paolo, and Paolo's son Fabio, and Oliverotto, were immediately set upon by Micheletto de Corella and his men and tied up. The Orsini were put aside until Cardinal Orsini in Rome and his brother Giulio Orsini could be stopped by Alexander. Oliverotto and Vitelli were tried during the night. They begged for their lives but when found guilty were seated back-to-back and strangled. When word that the Orsini in Rome had been arrested, the Orsini at Senigallia were murdered. The Orsini in Rome were poisoned, although the cardinal's death was described as being by natural causes. When Julius II took power a priest came forward and confessed to the poisoning, under orders from Alexander. The man, Asquino de Colloredo, spoke of the infallible white powder the Borgia used in all of their masked assassinations.

So ended what is known today as the Revolt of the Condottieri.

CHAPTER TEN

THE RENAISSANCE WARS

Alexander VI, Julius II, Emperor Maximilian I, Ferdinand of Spain, Louis XII, Henry VIII, François I, Emperor Charles V, Alessandro de' Medici, Clement VII

The origins of the Renaissance Wars was the Holy League formed by Alexander to rid Italy of Charles VIII, but as most of what happens during the Renaissance Wars takes place after Cesare's death, you can skip to the next chapter if you so wish, although this chapter does provide the occasion to bring to a tidy end the events that followed the disappearance of Alexander and Cesare. It also introduces Alessandro de' Medici, one of the world's most outlandish miscreants.

The expansion of Venice over the centuries had made enemies, and as Venice, like a spoiled child, always decided what was best for itself, a city-state either won against Venice or lost and gave in: there was no intermediary negotiation. The Venetians didn't hesitate to align themselves with the Ottomans when they felt their commerce--a lifeline without which they would cease to exist--was threatened. After all, one of their most vital possessions, Cyprus, was in spitting distance of Turkey. At the same time, Venice always found a reason not to come to the aid of this or that pope, or an invading force from France or Spain, unless the Serenissima could reap easy benefits.

The Venetians had thusly made enemies. Strangely, it was in the surrounding territories they ruled that the rural classes, the farmers, supported them because the Venetians were vultures of a far less aggressive nature than the nobles in places like Padua, Verona and Vicenza, whom the farmers found far more arrogant than the Venetians and who, especially, taxed them to death.

As all the great powers had lost something to the Serenissima, they met to form the League of Cambrai to get everything back:

Louis XII, the Roman Emperor Maximilian, the city-states of Mantua and Ferrara, and Pope Julius II, Alexander's successor, who wanted to recapture the totality of the Papel States.

When the Venetians learned of the League of Cambrai and knew for certain that an invasion was eminent, they closed ranks and raised the money needed for an army.

The French were the first to "enter the dance," as the French themselves put it, with the Battle of Agnadello. They came with their own men but also wanted Swiss mercenaries. While the cantons met to decide whether or not to participate, the French went over their heads, directly to the Swiss mercenaries themselves. They thought that all they needed were adequate bribes, and bribes did secure them several thousand mercenaries who needed the money, but not the expert forces provided by the cantons who, tired of being treated like rednecks by the French, refused to participate. The Swiss, like the Venetians, would always march to a different drummer, then as today.

The Venetians were drubbed at Agnadello, especially as they refused to commit their entire forces, saving a large number to protect their island kingdom, where they now withdrew. With incredible intelligence, they advised towns like Verona, Padua and Vicenza to surrender to the Holy Roman Emperor Maximilian, knowing that they would be able to win these places back, later, far more easily than if they surrendered to the French.

So the Venetians found themselves back home, but with their military largely intact, while all around them the farmers, who preferred them to the nobles who had now resumed power over them, began guerilla tactics against the invaders--the French and the troops of Maximilian--who were just beginning to arrive.

The Venetian genius continued when the Serenissima unilaterally gave back every position they had held, including everything Pope Julius II wanted. They did the same with their Spanish positions, the Venetian ports surrounding Naples, and they didn't even wait for Ferdinand of Spain to contact them, they sent embassies to *him* revealing their decision. They tried to do the same with Maximilian but failed. Both Pope Julius and King Ferdinand decided that a vital, living Venice would serve them better against the unbeatable French, and so they united their forces to reduce the power of Louis XII. That left only Maximilian as a major player in Louis' corner. Deeply religious, Maximilian would not fight against the pope, and when Ferdinand assured Maximilian that Maximilian's own son, Charles, would rule over Spain on the 20th birthday, Maximilian returned to the comforts of Vienna. Venice then took back Padua and Vicenza as they had foreseen, leaving only Verona in the hands of Louis. The pope got the Swiss cantons to provide him with 6,000 men, the best fighting force in Europe, men he paid extremely well, men he put aside as a spearhead should one be needed.

Then a coup de théâtre: Julius, afraid of Louis XII's growing power, proved himself to be the warrior pope History would crown him as being by breathing new life into the Holy League. Amazingly, incredibly, it would consist of Venice. Julius, who just basically wanted the Venetians to remain neutral, only asked the Serenissima to give the League the soldiers they wished to volunteer. Ferdinand of Spain would provide most of the troops and even Henry VIII was invited, Ferdinand promising him his aid in Aquitaine, a huge chunk of France vital to the English. It was announced that the League was absolutely not aimed at Louis, although it was.

The next year's campaign, that of 1511, in the absence of Louis who remained in France, was marked by Louis' men's attack on Brescia and the horrible sack of the town that was to follow. The attack took place in torrential rain and the French sustained many casualties. French infantry consisted mostly of Gascons and landsknechts, the dregs of humanity, who massacred and raped over a period of five days. Around 4,000 cartloads of stolen goods left the burning town, the soldiers now so rich that many simply returned home to France. The result was satisfying in the sense that the next town, Bergamo, paid the French 60,000 ducats to escape the same fate.

The next battle saw Spanish and papal forces against the French at Ravenna, said to have been the costliest massacre in troops in centuries. Perhaps 20,000 men and boys lost their lives, with a French win thanks to French cavalry, but with the loss of the cream of the French nobility. Cardinal Giovanni de' Medici, the future Leo X, was taken prisoner. But the French had been weakened and Julius and his Swiss mercenaries, aided by the Venetians, chased Louis' troops from Milan where they installed Massimiliano Sforza. Louis' troops went back to France. It was 1511. Forty-eight years of wars still remained.

Venice more or less leaves the scene as the Serenissima had suffered more than in its entire history--during the wars the Venetian town of Vicenza, for example, had changed hands 36 times, bringing massacre to the people with each upheaval, death, famine and rape, a fate worse than Hell itself.

Ferdinand now died, leaving the Spanish throne to Maximilian's son Charles, age 15. When Maximilian died, his son Charles, thanks to his pugnacity and intelligence, became the most important person of his times, King of Spain, Naples and Sicily, and Holy Roman Emperor. Louis XII died while honoring his new bride, Henry VIII's sister, perhaps a bit young and demanding for the old man. He was replaced by his son François I.

Julius died, replaced by the Medici Leo X who brought Florence back into the Medici lap. Spanish troops helped bring this about by sacking Prato, a town that had been sold to Florence in 1351 by Naples, a landmark massacre during which 6,000 were killed, a massacre remembered by Pratoans to this very day, summed up in a letter by an Italian to a friend, "Oh God, oh God, oh God, what cruelty!" The Florentines paid the Spanish 80,000 ducats to escape the same fate, with an additional 20,000 to the Spanish general.

The year was 1519 and there were still 40 years of inhuman suffering before the end of the Renaissance Wars.

In 1520 François decided to destabilize the very young Charles by backing revolts among the Länder in Germany and dissident followers of Martin Luther. Charles, very religious, united with Pope Leo X to rid Italy of the French by naming Massimiliano's brother, Francesco Sforza, Duke of Milan. Leo felt that Charles would be the best bulwark against Luther, and confirmed his hold over Naples. As the Swiss cantons were split over aid to François and to Leo, both king and pope received several thousand mercenaries. Venice was obliged by treaty to aid François, and sent troops, but under anonymity.

Because the French had never been welcome rulers of Milan, and because the Venetians took the first opportunity to flee the city, the fall of Milan was immediate. But then Leo X died and papal funding of the war evaporated, bringing havoc as every city-state used the vacuum of power to free itself from any foreign presence.

Order came when Charles proved himself intellectually and militarily invincible. He would be a great king, but in his wake thousands of men and boys, women and children, would have their lives snuffed out. Then François I, incapable of leaving well enough alone, invaded Italy. He was captured by Charles at Pavia and shipped to Spain.

François I and his huge nose.

François, who had already lost his virginity to his sister at age 10, was a lad 6 ½ feet tall and so big some girls couldn't accommodate him although most tried, and, it was said, virgins lined up around his bed awaiting their chance to be deflowered-- his specialty. His bed even accompanied him while he was out hunting, using it between kills, to the utter amazement of Henry VIII who had accompanied the king during his visit to France (Henry went far in such things, very far even, but not *that* far). François took whomever he wanted from the nobility, whether the ladies liked it or not, and apparently not all did as one woman had her husband infect himself with syphilis before infecting her so she could infect the king. Another woman had her face slashed, which didn't dissuade François as it wasn't her face that interested him.

The Treaty of Madrid gained François his freedom, but as he never envisaged respecting it, we won't go into its clauses except to say that the king was replaced by his two sons, both traumatized for life by the ordeal of their imprisonment.

Another League was formed, this one the League of Cognac, comprised of the new pope, another Medici, Clement VII, as well as François I, Henry VIII, Florence and Francesco of Milan. Charles was invited, but as the intent of the League was his covert overthrow, he couldn't very well join in. The aim, for Clement VII, was to place Naples--in the hands of Charles--under papal direction. François had joined the League as a bargaining chip to play in his hand with Henry VIII and his hand with Charles. For Henry, the League was nothing but papal wind, but as he needed Clement to give him a divorce from Catherine of Aragon, Charles's aunt, he went along.

Then, on all sides, things began to go horribly wrong. Charles's troops, a huge percentage of which were mercenaries, were unpaid and reduced to scavenge for food. The papal forces disbanded because neither Henry nor François believed in the viability of the League, and Venice, as usual, withdrew its men in order to save them should Venice itself be attacked. Florentines, again unhappy under Medici rule, held back funds (throughout all History one could ultimately be certain that, in the end, one could never count on Florence for anything, Florence eternally absent). With disorder everywhere, Charles's troops took things in hand by moving to Rome, which they sacked. The doors of the city were closed to Charles's troops but his seasoned warriors had no trouble scaling the walls, slaughtering any man, woman or child that came in reach. As many, if not most, of the landsknechts were Lutheran, churches were especially designated targets in which the usual filth was etched in the frescoes, a landsknecht pope was elected and nuns repeatedly raped on the altars, good sport for these husky lads deprived of warmth, food, pillage and sex during the preceding seemingly never-ending winter.

Charles was responsible. His lack of authority and failure to pay the troops on time led to his total loss of control over them. The sack went on for *eight months*, until there was literally nothing more to steal and no one undamaged enough to be worth raping. To Charles's wretched troops were added thousands more, any peasant from the surrounding countryside who wanted in on the spoils. An estimated 12,000 people were killed and the population of Rome, due to the murders and those who fled the town, fell from 55,000 to 10,000 after the sack. Nearly all of the pope's Swiss guard was slain, an event commemorated to this day by the Michelangelo-clad boys who have descended from them.

Charles reestablished control and made a treaty with Clement VII. His troops left Rome and the pope left Castel Sant'Angelo where he had taken cover. He would later crown Charles Holy Roman Emperor in Bologna, at age 30, the last pope to do so. Facing religious unrest at home, Charles made peace with François. The Medici pope Clement VII had Charles promise to restore Medici rule over Florence by marrying his daughter to the Florentine Alessandro de' Medici. Francesco Sforza remained Duke of Milan. Clement recognized Charles's right to Naples. Venice got back some land and Ferrara lost some. François's sons were freed from Spain. Peace broke out. The treaty, called the Treaty of Barcelona, was signed in 1529. But 30 more years of havoc remained.

As just mentioned, Charles promised to restore Medici rule over Florence by marrying his daughter to the Florentine Alessandro de' Medici. This boy is so unique, and of such interest, that we are now going to make a detour into his life and times.

Alessandro de' Medici, son of Pope Clement VII

Alessandro de' Medici was given rule over Florence by his father Pope Clement VII, the former Giulio di Giuliano de' Medici. Alessandro took advice from no one, living for his own pleasure, his motto being "They made me duke, so I'll enjoy it!" By enjoying it he meant wandering the streets at night fully armed, pushing aside anyone in his way, looking for a fight he was destined to win for the simple reason that he had barred the carrying of a sword or a firearm, both of which never left him, nor did his dagger. And he had reason to fear, as the nobility of Florence wanted him replaced by legitimate blood, noble blood. He had gained power at age 19 and had by now fully tasted every perversion, so that what was left was taking the hymen of those who still had one, notably nuns, and that of those who kept guard over theirs, virtuous women. He liked his boys too, for quick, easy couplings, as heated and virile as possible. His favorite companion was his cousin Lorenzino with whom he shared his bed and more when not extinguished from a night of whoring. And when he awoke with a lustful urge, Lorenzino was always conveniently spread out, naked, at his side. This is how Cellini had caught them many times, as the artist was permitted to come and go as he wished, and as Alessandro had no modesty and no need to hide his vices, Cellini was aware of everything that went on. "Meanwhile I went on making the Duke's portrait and oftentimes I found him napping after dinner with that Lorenzino of his," wrote Cellini in his autobiography (5).

Lorenzino, at times, behind his back, was called Lorenzaccio, "bad Lorenzo," for his habit of cutting off the heads of statues and other misdemeanors, clear proof that he shared much of Alessandro's waywardness, at least at the beginning. No one knows why Lorenzino turned against Duke Alessandro, aided by a professional assassin, Scoronconcolo. Some believe he wanted Florence to become a Republic again. Others suggest that he was just jealous of the duke's powers and privileges. As Duke Alessandro was hated, he was never without his body armor, weapons and guards. But Lorenzino told him that he had found a Florentine lady of exception beauty and, especially, ironclad virtue, who had been abandoned by her husband. Lorenzino would bring her to the duke, and from then on it was up to the duke to prove that he could triumph over virtue. Lorenzino convinced the duke to dismiss the guards for the night, to take off his armor and to slip naked into bed. From then on it was easy for Lorenzino to strike him with a dagger. Afterwards he rode off to Venice, a glove covering a finger Alessandro had nearly bitten off. There, he published his version of what had taken place in his *Apologia*, claiming to be a second Brutus. Lorenzino himself was later stabbed to death by a poisoned dagger on a bridge in Venice.

Charles tried to get Italian states to join him in a league, the purpose of which was their protection in exchange for yearly financial backing. In this Charles was the original mafia boss offering security in exchange for ransom. But there was a second purpose: to show to François that Charles had plenty of friends, and so France would do well to watch its step.

Paul III became pope and welcomed Charles to Rome with full honors, as Charles was now the most powerful prince in the world and the pope could benefit from his reflected glory. Paul initiated a meeting in Nice between Charles and François, with Paul officiating. The kiss of peace was exchanged. Pope Paul had another brilliant idea. He got his son, Pier Luigi Farnese, to offer Charles 2,000,000 ducats for Milan that Pier Luigi wanted for *his* son, Ottavio Farnese, who was already Charles's son-in-law, having married Charles's daughter Margaret, Alessandro de' Medici's widow. Charles was tempted to accept the 2,000,000 ducats for Milan, and in truth he should have as it was the destiny of Milan to be an eternal headache.

While this was going on François was busy trying to conquer Nice using French and Ottoman troops, to the disbelief of Christian Europe. François had even turned over the French natural port of Toulon to Barbarossa, a bloodthirsty murderer of Christian children and women, only second to the Great Khan. Charles sent Spanish ships to reinforce Nice, thusly thwarting François's plans. To avenge himself, François decided to return to reclaim Milan. Thrilled at the call of battle, infinitely more exciting than the call of the hunt, French boys, mostly still adolescents, begged their king for permission to join his ranks, and François naturally agreed. Frenchmen met Spaniards on Italian soil at Ceresole, the French seconded by Swiss mercenaries, the Spanish by Germans. There was even a crop of new Florentine lads, Cesare-Borgia clones, there in favor of Charles. The weapons of choice were harquebusiers and pistoliers, lances and pikes and arrows. The French and the Swiss were the most redoubtable, and soon the Spanish and the Germans were throwing down their arms and seeking shelter among the horses of the French cavalry, the cavalry deemed more humane than the Swiss and French troops who were mercilessly ending the lives of all who crossed their path. Around 15,000 of Charles's men were said to have died, a drop in the bucket in what the Spanish and the Florentines and the Germans and the Swiss had still to offer in the endless generations nurtured on soil drenched in blood.

While awaiting this new generation of cannon fodder, Charles and François signed the Peace of Crépy where all territories taken since their meeting at Nice would be returned. Thousands of sacrificed lives for absolutely nothing. A marriage between Charles and François's offspring was set for some unspecified future.

The year was 1547. Twelve years remained of the Renaissance Wars.

Then François I and Henry VIII died. François's son, the future Henry II, was a good boy and king, but no François. Henry's son Edward VI was a good boy too, but dead at age 16, replaced by his sister Mary who wedded Charles V's son Philip (another good boy but, alas, in no way his father). Not until Elizabeth would England be a problem again to the Spanish, or to anyone else.

Through lack of testosterone-charged leaders, Europe would know some peace. But other boys like the Borgia brothers, Juan and Cesare, beautiful and virile, were on the horizon, as will eternally be the case.

Unfortunately, the Spanish missed their unique chance when they had imprisoned François's son, the future Henry II. How easy it would have been too spoil the lad, to flatter his ego, to respect his nobility. Instead, he was ill-treated, and as such he hated the Spanish with all his heart and soul, enough to continue his relations with the Ottomans, enough to bring death to still untold thousands.

What took place next were tiny disputes in localities with names such as Brà, Bene, Asti and others. Charles took Siena and lost it and took it back. The Sienese were reduced to such misery that Charles ruled over a city of skeletons, a city known then, as it is today, as one of the most civilized and cultured in Italy. Charles signed over power to Philip who was good at what he did but, as said, no Charles. The French did take Corsica, for a while, before taking it permanently in 1769, making Napoleon French, to the apparent joy of French mothers who would witness their sons, thousands upon thousands of them, sacrifice their brief lives *pour la gloire de la patrie.*

Charles V, François I and Julius II left the stage, and the stage went silent.

Peace came with the Treaty of Cateau-Cambrésis. The year was 1559. The Renaissance Wars were over.

CHAPTER ELEVEN

THE STAGE GOES SILENT
Alexander VI, Cesare Borgia, Gianbattista Ferrari, Giovanni Michiel, the family d'Este, Micheletto, Pius III, Julius II, Queen Isabella of Spain, Juan of Navarre

In order to continue his conquests Cesare needed evermore money. New cardinals were nominated, raising 130,000 ducats. Cardinal Gianbattista Ferrari became ill owing to, according to rumor, the Borgia white powder. Alexander had his residence emptied of its gold and jewels, bringing him 80,000 ducats. Ferrari had been hated as he had helped no one but himself. He was so avaricious, went the story, that he refused to pay St. Peter 1,000 ducats as entry into Heaven. He refused, too, to pay the lesser fee of 500. He even refused the 1 ducat that St. Peter requested, after which the furious saint told him to ''Go to Hell!'' which was, apparently, exactly what Ferrari had deserved all along. Cardinal Giovanni Michiel died after ''a strange session of vomiting.'' His home was plundered of its goods, worth 150,000 ducats.

Cesare was no fool. He knew his father would not live on forever. He had thusly looted Italy of every ducat seizable, he had storerooms of weapons at his disposal and his troops loved this handsome fearless man who conceded their every wish as long as they remained loyal to him. What he hadn't counted on was *his* nearly dying at exactly the same time as his father, which is precisely what happened. What he hadn't counted on either was the election of a new pope even more vigorous, intelligent and belligerent than Alexander VI.

Cesare and his father had been invited to a banquet after which they both fell seriously ill.

Illness was nothing new to the Renaissance. All the actors in this book, all without exception, had fallen ill multiple times throughout their lives. Lucrezia, for example, was continuously sick--especially following her many miscarriages. Illness came from literally everywhere, bad food, incredibly diseased water that one drank or swam in; illness came from common flue, from typhus, cholera and malaria; from flees and rats and dogs and other people. It came through breathing, sweating, defecating and fucking. Illness favored the months of July and August, hot muggy months propitious to dysentery. All of Alexander's predecessors, Innocent, Sixtus, Pius and Calixtus had died during those months. And it was now July, "the month," Alexander had said, "when fat men croak," and both he and Cesare were at death's door. Perhaps they believed, as did the people, that they had been poisoned during the banquet. Perhaps, as some said, they themselves had tried to poison their host, an ever-criticizing cardinal they both could well do without--and his money they could well do with, but somehow they had drunk their own means of murder. As Alexander was now seventy-three, he was in more danger than his young son. They were both bled although, unlike his father, Cesare was plunged into cold water, the accepted cure for fever. Alexander received last rites but not Cesare, a former cardinal, who vaunted his atheism.

Was Alexander guilty of some of the most heinous crimes known to humanity--even the sexual assault on Astorre Manfredi and his fifteen-year-old brother, before ordering them strangled and thrown into the Tiber? Or, as one recent source claims, did he die a misunderstood saint? There is only one response: God will know His own. Let Him decide who goes into the eternal flames or gets access to the 72 virgins. As for me, I've spent a lot of time reading about this unique creature without whom--and without miscreants like him--history would be a far more boring concern. But ... one does not touch children. If there is no eternal punishment for those who harm lads, lads as innocent as Astorre and the 8,000 Srebrenicans so recently slain, then what does life represent other than a moment of often sublime beauty on a planet of sublime beauty, in the arms, if one is lucky, of he who warms your bed and whose beauty brings tears to your eyes?

Alexander died and Cesare's first order was to send Micheletto de Corella to his father's rooms where, putting a knife to the throat of its guardian, Cardinal Casanova, he obliged him to disclose the places Alexander had hidden, *à la Volpone*, his gold and jewels, worth, wrote the Venetian ambassador Giustinian, 500,000 ducats. In his haste Micheletto overlooked rings and a tiara that the servants found and stole, as they stole his clothes, furniture, bedding, drapes and tapestries. When the cardinals made an inventory later, they came up with a further 25,000 ducats in gems and gold, said Burchard. Burchard, as Master of Ceremonies, was responsible for the pope's burial. He had to hide the fact that even the pope's rings had been wrenched from his fingers. Alexander's body was placed in the usual papal triple coffin (the first, cypress, a simple wood signifying he is an ordinary human being; the second, lead, is engraved with his name and the years of his pontificate; and the last, elm, is rare and precious and signifies his dignity). As customary, paid paupers carried his remains, swollen and black, reported Burchard, to St. Peter's where the body was abandoned, no one even taking the time, apparently, to light a vigil of candles. Such was Alexander's nefarious reputation for being close to the devil that holy water was said to have boiled when poured into his mouth, steaming up the chamber. He stank intolerably and, Burchard maintains, he was erect there where he had been erect all his life.

Nearly overnight Cesare lost it all. What remained of the Orsini, and they were numerous, arrived in Rome at the head of 1,200 armed men. Cesare's palaces were sacked and the lands he had conquered were recovered by the counts, lords, dukes and princes he had overturned. Still deathly ill, he was carried away by litter to recuperate at his sister's retreat of Nepi, where he found his mother Vannozza and his brother Jofrè. Giuliano della Rovere entered Rome for the conclave, surrounded by his own army of crossbowmen, despite Micheletto that Cesare had sent at the head of a hit team to kill him. The Venetian ambassador Giustinian was commissioned to ask Cesare to remove his men from Castel Sant'Angelo which had been taken by Micheletto de Corella's troops. In return, he was promised to be confirmed in all of his functions. In Rome Pius III was elected, a good man who at age 21 had been archbishop of Siena. Among the cardinals was Ippolito d'Este, he who, before riding off to Rome, had been laying Sancia, along with his brother Alfonso, Lucrezia's husband, both at the same time, although perhaps not at the same time in the same bed. As for Lucrezia, she was growing out of her tastes for young handsome males, in favor of what Italy had in literati. In Rome Ippolito bedded Cesare's favorite mistress, left alone while he was at Nepi. No one, and especially Pius III, trusted Cesare, and no one wanted him back in Rome. But Pius III received his envoys and fell for Cesare's assurances that he wished to return simply to die in the holy city. Pius allowed his return, only to find Cesare in perfect health. But this too was an act performed in the presence of Pius, as Cesare was still so ill that after the meeting he returned to his palace and to bed where he would remain for some weeks. His situation worsened when, learning that he was not going to follow Alexander in death as the court physicians had assured everyone, the Colonna and the Orsini decided to move against him. At the same time, he was losing his hold over his own troops who, despite their love for him, were demanding their pay.

Then Destiny stepped in again. Pius died ten days after his coronation, granted eternal rest by one of the followers of his replacement, Borgia white powder employed to make way for the powerful Julius II, one of life's never-ending incongruities, in that it was the Borgias means of death that brought their mortal enemy to power (the poisoning of Pius was, historically, nothing more than a rumor in a court ruled by rumors). The conclave, which had felt itself so threatened that it met in the fortified Castel Sant'Angelo, lasted part of a single day, the shortest in history. Julius won over the Spanish cardinals by promising to reinstate Cesare, of Spanish origin, in all his functions. He won over the Italian cardinals because they were split, Orsini against Colonna, and Julius made them believe that a French pope, in this case George d'Amboise, would take the papacy back to Avignon. Besides reinstating Cesare in all his functions, Rovere promised Cesare that the three-year-old daughter Cesare had never seen would marry thirteen-year-old Francesco della Rovere, heir to Guidobaldo da Montefeltro who was, you may remember, impotent (whose wife had loyally stated that she'd rather have him as a brother than as a lover). In addition, Rovere promised that Cesare would have access to the money he had stashed in banks in Genoa. Cesare knew he would eventually lose the Romagna, but he believed he would nonetheless remain a man of wealth and power.

Strong in body and mind, intelligent, handsome, arrogant and utterly ruthless, the new pope had contracted syphilis but with age he replaced the lust of the loins with that of the stomach, devoting himself to roast pig and strong wines. His temperament was described as melancholic, capable of the greatest furies. He created the Swiss Guard and put Michelangelo to work on the Sistine Chapel (and the Guard's uniforms). He refused Henry VIII's divorce, ending the Catholic Church in England, and he brought war and peace to the continent according to his whims, and was only prevented from uniting Italy into one country by the emergence of someone still more powerful than he, the Grim Reaper.

But for the moment, Julius was only 59 and in perfect health. As a boy he had worked on a cargo boat shipping onions up and down the Italian coast. At 27 he had been made a cardinal by Sixtus IV, one of the six nephews so honored--although Sixtus had the habit of passing off his sons as nephews too. He was no scholar and when Michelangelo suggested a statue of him holding a book, one of the many statues that were to adorn his tomb, he told the sculptor to replace the book by a sword.

Julius, as Machiavelli had foreseen, kept none of his promises. A wagon train of Cesare's wealth was stopped and seized in Bologna, and turned back under papal escort to Rome. His money in Genoa was blocked while Julius did the paperwork to retrieve it from the banks there. Micheletto was stopped outside Ferrara at the head of a mule train carrying the gold and jewels Cesare had stolen from the Vatican and were now destined for safe keeping by his sister Lucrezia. Florence refused Cesare safe passage so that he could go north to France where his young wife awaited him and where he could find safety under Louis XII. Julius then issued a warrant for his arrest, accusing him of the murders of his brother Juan, his sister's husband Alfonso, Astorre Manfredi and Astorre's brother, as well as Vitelli and Oliverotto garroted in Senigallia, the two Orsini strangled in Rome, the Orsini cardinal poisoned, Varano and his sons, and others. But in exchange for his giving up the wealth he had hoarded and the fortifications in the Romagna still in possession of those who remained loyal to him, Cesare was allowed exile in Spain.

He retired to Chinchilla, a mountain castle in the heights near Valencia. Machiavelli blamed all of Cesare's disasters on his original agreement to back Julius's bid for the papacy, after Julius had promised him that he could retain his papal functions, his army and the Romagna. Machiavelli could not understand how someone as intelligent as Cesare could have done something so stupid. Others around Cesare suggested that his illness had adversely affected his brain.

Cesare's rout was such that even King Louis XII, who had called him his dear son, sent word to Ferrara and Alfonso, Lucrezia's husband, that he was free to leave her, as France no longer recognized her as being his legitimate wife. Luckily for Lucrezia, Alfonso had grown to love her, and this despite the fact that she had never stopped welcoming lovers into her bed (as he too was doing). Other scandals continued to haunt her. One of Alfonso's brothers, Ippolito, who was in the conclaves that elected Pius III and Julius II, a cardinal of unbounded lustfulness, had fallen in love with a local beauty. The girl claimed that she far preferred another of Ippolito's brothers, Giulio, whose beautiful brown eyes alone were worth more than all of Ippolito. In response the cardinal waylaid his brother and tried to cut out those wonderful eyes. Alfonso forced Ippolito to ask for pardon, but as Giulio suffered horrible pain and the near total loss of sight, he decided to get revenge on both brothers, Alfonso and Ippolito, by having them killed. He united his forces with still another of his brothers, Ferrante. Their conspiracy was discovered, however, and although Alfonso would not have them executed, he did send them to prison. Ferrante died in his dungeon forty-three years later, Giulio endured for fifty-three.

Caterina Riario Sforza de' Medici gave herself to Christ, while Lucrezia, despite ever-increasing amounts of donations to convents and churches as she grew older, never abandoned that part of herself that wanted to be a woman to men of flesh and blood. Right up to the end she continued affairs with men, the two most important being Francesco Gonzaga, ruler of Mantua, and Pietro Bembo, writer, historian and poet, for whom she wrote letters of stupefying sensuality (for the period).

Right up to the finish line she continued to give Alfonso children, five in all. At age thirty-nine she died giving birth, birth to a child and birth to a star, her star, that shines as brightly now as it did 500 years ago, solid proof that it is better to use life and be used by it than to flee the storm, dodging the droplets, seeking an illusive shelter that exists, in the end, for none of us.

In the mountain retreat of Chinchilla things went wrong for Cesare when his exile turned into captivity. Isabella of Spain decided to follow Julius's lead in prosecuting him for the deaths of his brother Juan, duke of Gadía, and Lucrezia's husband, Alfonso of Aragon, both of Spanish lineage. He escaped from his castle by climbing down a rope. He made his way by boat and trek to Pamplona in Navarre, to his brother-in-law Juan of Navarre where he reunited with his wife and the child he'd never seen. Juan put him at the head of his troops. Because the city-states in Spain were in incessant upheaval, just like their Italian counterparts, Cesare was constantly at war. His last day found him chasing a band of rebels. At age thirty-one he was still in the full glory of his bravado and virility and so thought nothing of outdistancing his men. Alas, the rebels he was chasing turned to face him and, highly outnumbered, he received many blows, one of which was the fatal plunge of a dagger to his throat, just above the armor. He fell into a ravine, just like Caterina's stable boy husband, Feo; he was stripped naked as Feo had been; but his genitals had not been mutilated, as Feo's. His were covered by a rock by one of the attackers who recognized him. Juan of Navarre had the body buried in the small church of Viana, where it lies to this day.

Cesare was a man of his times, violent and choleric, imminently Italian is his duplicity, deceit and cunning, whose charisma was such that his legend and bravura have spanned 500 years. A man, not just of his time, but of all time.

Cesare by Sebastiano del Piombo

PART II

CESARE BORGIA

HIS VIOLENT TIMES

CHAPTER TWELVE

PERKIN
Perkin Warbeck, Simnel, Margaret of Burgundy, Richard III, Edward IV Henry VII, Maximilian I, Philip I, War of the Roses, James IV, Ferdinand and Isabella, Charles VIII

The story of Simnel and Perkin is as true as one can make it after half a millennium. It's a passionate tale that involves five very lonely people: A boy who lost his father and his brother, and was himself purportedly assassinated at age 9: Richard, son of

Edward IV. A tale of another lad, abandoned young to his fate, whose love of beautiful clothes--a setting for his own beauty--would lead to the loss of his handsome head, a lad born with the name Perkin. A woman, Margaret of Burgundy, wife of Charles the Bold and sister of King Edward IV and Richard III, whose only request of life was the birth of a baby she herself could not bear, but who found her consolation in adopting two other lads, two pretenders, Simnel and Perkin. A king, James of Scotland, whose father died in war and who spent his childhood seeking another. And, finally, a king marked by the loss of his father at an early age, a king who fought tooth and nail for a kingdom and won it thanks to the death of the boys in the Tower, King Henry VII.

Richard, Duke of York, second son of Edward III, and his brother Edward, were smothered by their uncle, their father's brother, Richard III, in the most vile murder English royalty has known, the murder of two children. Little Richard and his brother Edward V had been locked in the Tower of London. As Edward was the older he guessed the fate awaiting them both, and despite Richard's trying to entice him into play, he grew each day more saturnine. When the end did come, in the midst of the night, it was Edward who was thankfully asleep, while Richard, seizing immediately the purpose of the men who stole into the boys' chambers, begged them to take him and permit his brother the king to live. The assassins took both. Richard III was later killed in battle, his soul exposed each time one opens Shakespeare to read of his dastardly deed, the robbing of two boys of their precious lives.

Perkin, the boy who would be chosen by Yorkists to replace the smothered Richard, was spotted, in Ireland, during a festival on which the usual sumptuary laws did not apply. Decked out in superb doublet and beautiful black gown, news of his beauty and countenance brought his attention to those who wished to undo the King of England in favor of the Yorkists, in battle against the Lancastrians for generations. The boy refused his being taken for royalty, refusal upon refusal until the awe and respect of those who had approached him--he whose parents had set him on his own like a wandering gypsy from childhood--gradually succumbed to their impressments. The task was herculean in its vastness: He would have to learn manners and princely comportment. He would need the Latin learned as a child by the real Richard and the English language the real Richard had spoken since birth. He would need to know the lives of his father, King Edward IV, and his mother, as well as those of their advisers and his and his brother's servants. He would need to know his daily routine from the moment he awoke to the moment he retired.

It was the sitting king, Henry VII, who would have to unmask the lad, a lad already accepted by the French king Charles VIII--who received the boy at his court and shared his mistresses with him, no big affair for Charles who prided himself on never having the same woman twice, even if he was the ugliest monarch in living memory. The lad was recognized as being legitimate by the Roman Emperor Maximilian and his son Philip, about the same age as the pretender, as was Charles, all three around 24, and on friendly terms with him.

Henry VII was the monarch who founded the Tudors, ending--with the death of Richard III at Bosworth--the War of the Roses that had bled England white for generations. He would impose 24 years of relative peace on his country, followed by his son Henry VIII, whose years were those of dissension and death. He married Edward IV's daughter Elizabeth, unifying his red rose to her white rose. An act of genius immediately followed. He declared himself king a day *before* the Battle of Bosworth, thus allowing him to proclaim that those who had fought against him had been traitors, allowing him to confiscate their lands, castles and their goods, followed, after his coronation, by a decree stating that any of the traitors who would swear fealty to him could have their possessions back. Edward IV had had two bothers, Richard who became Richard III, now dead, and Clarence. Clarence had been convicted of treason and executed. But Clarence had a son, Edward, a possible threat to Henry VII because of blood more noble than Henry's. He was put away in the tower. Later Edward would share his cell and his bed (a usage of the times) with Perkin, and plot with the boy to overthrow Henry VII. For this Edward would be beheaded, a fascinating story for another book.

The plot thickened when a lad named Simnel appeared to claim that he was Edward, Clarence's son. As the real Edward was being held in secret, a prisoner in the Tower, no one could dispute his assertion.

Simnel's real name has never come to light, but we do know that around age 10 he was taken under the wing of a priest, Richard Simon, who decided to make the handsome boy a king. The priest Simon was exceedingly erudite and taught the boy everything he would need to know about courtly behavior. Simon contacted Yorkists who found in Simnel the perfect tool to overthrow Henry VII. They began by spreading the rumor that Edward had escaped from the Tower and made his way to Dublin. It was in Dublin that Simnel was crowned King Edward VI (Edward IV's son, killed in the Tower by Richard III, had been Edward V). An army was mounted and various Yorkists went to Burgundy where Margaret of Burgundy, Edward's aunt, held power. She furnished 2,000 men who returned to England and met Henry's troops at the Battle of Stoke Fiend where they were defeated. Those not killed were executed except for Simons, saved due to his being a priest, although he was imprisoned for life. Incredibly, Henry felt that Simnel himself had been nothing more than a lad manipulated by adults. He made the boy a spit-turner in the royal kitchen, and later a falconer! The boy married and fathered a priest who exercised under Henry VIII.

Simnel

Eventually he turned up in Ireland where his love of sumptuous clothing brought him to the attention of Yorkists who convinced him to play the role of the smothered Richard, as mentioned. From Ireland he went to Margaret of Burgundy, sister of Edward IV and Richard III, who wanted the Yorkists back on the throne with such intensity that she undertook the education of Richard/Perkin, as she had done with Simnel. He learned the ways and the secrets of the court of England, and his aptitude for languages and personal beauty did the rest. Margaret sent him to James of Scotland.

What followed can only be described as a love affair between Richard/Perkin and King James IV, a true love affair, albeit not necessarily in a physical sense because we do know that both Richard/Perkin and James were ardent lovers of the opposite sex. Richard/Perkin had wandered through Europe as a child and his early adolescence had taken place in Portugal and the royal court of Portugal, known for its liberality in matters sexual, and the ardor of its boys and girls in sharing of their bodies. James was insatiable, sexually, as were so many males of position throughout Europe, satisfying himself with the girls--from servants to courtesans to ladies of royalty--who expected and desired his attention. The same was true of France, as Henry VIII was to learn thanks to Anne Boleyn and her sister, whom Henry had "known" long before Anne, girls brought up in the French court. Fingers, tongues and back passages were of no secret to even the youngest demoiselles in France and Portugal, while still maintaining an intact hymen. Boys adored showing off in skin-tight trousers, leaving nothing of their muscular buttocks to the imagination, and, in front, held in place by strings or buttons, were cod pieces of immense dimensions, as alluring to maidens as were the boys' gestures, their hands stroking the immense bulges.

As so often with boys at that time, James had lost his father to battle when very young, and literally went from man to man, afterwards, with the heart-breaking question, "Are you my father, sir?" Richard/Perkin had been set free from his father far too young, as had Henry VII whose father died in battle even before his birth. These men were drawn to their own through an absence that nothing in the world, nothing but one's only true father, can fill.

James, at 22, was just a few months older than Richard/Perkin. From the moment of Richard/Perkin's arrival James took him in hand, literally in hand in the sense that at every possible occasion, and especially in church, James entwined his hands in those of Richard, hands they joined in the worship and the presence of God. They ate together, perhaps not from the same plate as Richard Coeur de Lion and Philippe II, and they slept in the same bed, without the intimacy of the young and futures kings of England and France, Richard and Philippe (1).

James was generous to a fault although far from rich, but Richard/Perkin had nothing. After the mass, it was James who would make a contribution in the name of his friend. James was an athlete, but too trusting, as even his closest advisor, John Ramsay, was a spy in the pay of Henry VII. He was so concerned about his people that he would roam the countryside dressed as they, and seek lodging for the night amidst the most humble, all in an effort to learn what they thought of their king.

Lastly, James provided for his guest's needs by giving him the daughter of the wealthiest man in Scotland, Katherine Gordon, daughter of the Earl of Huntly. She was young, beautiful and virgin, and James saw to it that the marriage took place rapidly so that Richard/Perkin and she could enter into union. Later, a captive of Henry VII, Perkin was denied access to Katherine, the reason for his ill-considered actions, while Henry lusted for her but apparently did not take advantage of his limitless powers. James and Katherine would remain loyal to the boy to the end, even if James was forced to make certain concessions to Henry in order to save his country.

Perkin Warbeck

James and Richard/Perkin recognized in each other the brother neither had had, the shared resemblance of two boys of the same age, the need of masculine affection that no woman can ever fulfill in a man, the reason men defend each other to the death in war.

Naturally, everyone thought that with Richard/Perkin on the English throne they could, one and all, gain something of priceless value with Richard/Perkin in power: Margaret would have more say in the running of her Burgundy. The Roman Emperor Maximilian would have an English ally he could order around, as he could no longer do even his son Philip. And James would enjoy increased trade and more fluid relations with his neighbor England. But all said and done, James's chief motivation may well have been the beauty of his friendship with the boy-who-would-be-king.

James IV

It was James who insisted on invading England, and Ramsay, James's spy, reported to Henry that James, who loved joists and fighting with axes and swords and crossbows, was pushing the boy forward. But Richard/Perkin was not enthusiastic about an invasion because he *knew* the truth behind his right to the throne of England. And anyway, he had a new wife with lands and nobility and in September he would have a son. What was England now to him? He most resembled the Trojan Prince Paris, ensconced with Helen behind the impregnable walls of Troy. But like Troy, the Greeks were coming in the form of Henry VII (3).

One is nonetheless amazed by the backing Richard/Perkin benefited from: Maximilian and Burgundy under Maximilian's boy Philip; Margaret capable of offering vast sums of money; and a huge number of Yorkists and other supporters, all furnishing troops, horses and finances. A great number of Yorkists from England sent their seals to Richard as proof of their adherence to his plan of conquest. Alas, the seals were intercepted and forwarded to Henry who had most of the men, the cream of English nobility, beheaded. Only the very young were spared, if imprisonment for life can be so judged. Some did buy their way out, others had been truly loved by Henry and it was they who had no chance of being pardoned. Also, the sums invested by Henry in his defense were absolutely colossal. This was especially painful to a man who was one of history's original misers, amassing the greatest fortune England had ever known, money that would go to his son Henry VIII, making the boy, already lucky in looks and lucky in advisors, the richest lad in the world--

until the gods decided to tip the scales, although only at the very end of Henry VIII's miserable life.

On the sidelines of all of this were Ferdinand and Isabella, King and Queen of Spain, a couple who had loved each other the moment their eyes met. Their intelligence, in the sense of both brainpower as well as spies, was such that they knew the truth about the boy, and spent every hour trying to convince the world of the hoax, and thereby avoid useless wars. They brought order to government, they saved Spain from bankruptcy, they reduced crime for the first time in the country's history, and, icing on the cake, they sent Columbus on an excursion that would double the surface of the known world and enrich it beyond the grasp of the imagination.

At age six Isabella had been promised to Ferdinand but later it was suggested that she marry Edward IV of England or his brother the future Richard III, killer of infants, she held strong to her desire to wed Ferdinand. An obstacle to their union was their consanguinity, yet this was overcome by the Spanish Cardinal Borgia, the future Alexander VI. Her brother the king nevertheless disapproved, forcing her to escape to the wedding site, Valladolid, where she was joined by and married to Ferdinand, who had been disguised as a servant to avoid the king's army. When the king died she was crowned but for the first years she had to wage war against those who thought they had a better claim to the throne than she. Even Portugal invaded in an attempt to seize power. Her place finally became legitimized with the birth of a son.

Slavery was forbidden--hundreds of years before Lincoln--under Ferdinand and Isabella, but the interdict was little applied. The Inquisition was given full power and Jews were allowed three months to leave Spain with neither gold nor silver nor money nor arms nor horses. Half are thought to have converted, perhaps cosmetically. Muslims too were ordered to convert or get out.

Their daughter Joanna was married to the Roman Emperor Maximilian's son Philip, opening the door for Roman Empire rule over Spain. Their youngest daughter Catherine married Henry VIII's brother but he died, supposedly before consuming the marriage. Catherine went to Henry VIII himself, sowing the seeds for the destruction of the Catholic Church in England.

At Isabella's death she was entombed in a sepulcher built by the Roman Emperor Charles V, the new Charles I of Spain, Joanna and Philip's son. Ferdinand followed her, in the same chapel, a few years later.

The tomb of Ferdinand and Isabella

James's plan seems to have been to cross the border into England, grab a few border towns, and thanks to the uprising of the English people--especially Yorkists from the north--he would return home and let Richard/Perkin continue on to glory. Before setting off, both friends had signed an agreement under which certain English lands and towns would be given to Scotland, and 100,000 marks forwarded to James' coffers once the lad was on the throne (which would have reimbursed a huge number of church donations James had offered in Richard's name).

The border was crossed and James initiated a burned-earth policy that left Richard/Perkin in tears, claiming that James would leave him no one and nothing over which he could govern. Richard/Perkin rode off to the safety of Scotland and as Henry's troops approached, James did likewise.

Following the collapse of James's army, Maximilian kept doggedly at Richard/Perkin's side. Ferdinand and Isabella tried everything in their power to get the boy to Spain where they could pension him off, thereby neutering him. Maximilian's son Philip gave up on the boy and Margaret let Charles VIII take over for her, Charles who desperately wanted Richard as a joker to play in his wars with Henry. As for Ireland, it took Henry's bribes and turned its back on the lad.

Henry's troops approached Scotland. Henry offered James his daughter, age 6, in marriage, a peace offering. Although Henry did not hesitate to put traitors to death, he had a very enticing side, one that had forgiven Simnel, had paid for his marriage and had set the boy up as a falconer. And despite the hundreds of deaths occasioned by Perkin, despite the cost in today's money of millions to Henry, and a hunt that had gone on for six long years, despite all that Henry took the lad to his side, when finally captured, not as a son, but not far from being one either. And now Henry VII was offering his daughter, his own flesh and blood, to his enemy. But James refused to surrender his friend Perkin to what he believed was certain death. Yet as the wolves closed in on all sides, from Spain and especially from England, James had no choice but to ask his friend to leave, at the head of a small army, on an ill-named ship the *Cuckoo*, destination England where Richard/Perkin would become king. No one was present at their goodbyes, but I hope they were worthy of the sincere love and wondrous moments they had shared.

But Richard/Perkin was intercepted by Henry on the high seas and captured. Richard/Perkin became just Perkin.

Henry VII

As I stated at the beginning of this chapter, this is a tale of five unhappy people. Henry VII had been an only son, his father dead before his birth and no noble men to show him the route to manhood, let alone kinghood. He had no real pedigree, no real royal blood, and until the rise of Henry VIII such would remain the case. Affable, he was nonetheless a loner and would stay so until the end of his life. Perkin Warbeck had stood alone from an early age, and the story of the conditions of his passing from one adult to another, as he passed from one country to another, will remain unknown, but was certainly trying and forlorn. His thirst for betterment was mirrored in his choice of clothes, which in turn brought him to the attention of others who would use him as he had always, in one way or another, been used. He lost to Henry but in so doing he gained a wife and child, was welcomed to Henry's court, one lonely man in the service of another, and there he could have risen to heights less than a kingly Richard IV, but to an unimaginable prosperity, given his lowly birth. It was perhaps Henry's own lowly birth, in comparison with other Yorkists and Lancastrians, that allowed him an intimacy--albeit limited--with humbler lads such as Simnel and Perkin. In his own gauche way he tried to make friends of them both, but it is the Fates, not men, the ultimate arbiters of one's destiny. Henry was 41, the boy, as he called him, 22. Perkin confessed all, totally astonished at the king's leniency. Maximilian and Margaret had known of the conspiracy, Perkin admitted to Henry, no one else knew, and certainly not James. On bended knee the boy confessed, but his manner was remained noble. His wife was brought before Henry who was said to have lusted for her but had kept himself in check by sending Katherine to serve his queen, Elizabeth. Order had returned to the world, the planets again in their rightful orbits.

Maximilian requested Perkin's freedom, while Katherine, bless her, remained faithful to Perkin, even after Henry had divulged all, but although Henry allowed them to meet at court, in public, he kept them separated physically, his way, perhaps, of unmanning the lad.

The power of fucking has always totally amazed and captivated me. Where along the evolutionary line did something available to nearly every living thing on the planet become an obsession, to such an extent that psychologists say a boy is no longer controllable once he has wet his brush, as the French say (*se tremper le pinceau*). The concept rules the locker room, occupying every thinking moment and expression between young men, as I myself overheard, "I made her cum three times last night." Even the word fuck itself is the ultimate in the English language. In the throes of orgasm it's cried out, as it is when a lad hits his finger with a hammer. Here Henry unmanned the boy Perkin by separating him from his wife.

Perkin was free to roam the royal premises and the grounds, on foot or horse, accompanied by two unarmed guards that those not in the know took for his servants. Perkin was in fact so free of restraints that Henry had to defend himself by saying that the boy was indeed being punished, this to the obvious disbelief of those who had access to both men. Perkin slept in a small room near the king's and had a tailor paid by Henry. He was at court with Simnel, and one wonders if they were not looked down on, both just lowly fakes, after all, of lesser importance than the fire-eater or sword-swallower who, at least, both earned their keep through amusing the court. Perhaps they were both just tolerated because Henry tolerated them, and the king was the measure of all things. This humiliation, alone, with the humiliation of his being separated from Katherine, were becoming increasingly unbearable.

All hell broke out when he escaped. The king offered 100 pounds for his capture, a huge sum. The reasons for Perkin's escape are unknown: A need to physically reunite with Katherine, hatred at being penned up and exhibited, or perhaps Margaret and Maximilian had offered him exile as a free man. Henry was said to have been indifferent, and even though the boy had tried to usurp his place, had cost him a fortune, and had been the cause of the loss of thousands of lives, this may have become the case, although I doubt it.

He was caught four days later, totally undone, turned over by the monks from whom he had begged sanctuary. The end is painful to reveal. When Paris in Troy won a footrace, the crowds went wild in his favor because, said one, "the boy is young and beautiful and when offered the laurels, he wept"(3). Perkin too was young, just 23, and beautiful, but he lost, and as such he was put on exhibit before the people who spat on him. Few were those, like me, who had loved this boy for being the entirely unique lad who had kept the known world breathless: Ferdinand and

Isabella who with every exchange of letters begged their ambassadors to send more news of this Perkin; the Emperor of the Romans who dispatched a ship to his rescue the moment he learned of his flight; Charles VIII, King of France, jumping up and down with glee at Henry's embarrassment, beside himself with joy; and James of Scotland, on his knees before God whom he begged to save the life of his friend, unaware that God's chosen few had denied the boy sanctuary.

Contrary to popular belief, the Tower had more or less furnished rooms--the richness of which depended on the importance of the occupant--as well as cells. Perkin's was small, with a small bed, table and chair, and a window so small a single bar sufficed to make it escape proof. Some occupants had freedom of movement throughout the Tower. Perkin did not and may even have worn shackles and an iron neck collar. The cleanliness of the rooms, their salubriousness, depended too on the nobility of the inhabitant.

A delegation from Burgundy was sent by Margaret and Maximilian's son Philip in order to resolve certain questions between Henry and Burgundy, one of which was the health of Perkin, of upmost importance to Margaret. Ferdinand and Isabella's ambassador was invited to see the boy too, as the lad seems to have become an obsession to the Spanish. Henry himself escorted the lot to Perkin's room. In front of them Perkin admitted that he was a fake, news to none present but something Henry insisted on during every visit by outsiders. The Spanish ambassador claims Henry had had the boy disfigured, that he had beaten the last remnant of beauty out of him. In public Henry expressed his disgust of Maximilian and James, and his utter hatred of Margaret, the mastermind behind the entire hoax, according to him. It seems that Margaret wrote to Henry, abjectly demanding his pardon.

The reader may remember that on gaining power Henry had imprisoned Edward, the son of Clarence, brother of Edward IV and Richard III. He had been imprisoned because he had had a better claim to the throne than Henry himself. Since then, plots unceasingly came to Henry's ears concerning Yorkists who dreamed of having Edward on Henry's throne. Other plotters wanted to place Perkin on the throne, as his right to it, as Edward IV's son, was far stronger than Edward's. It had become obvious, for years, that Henry would never know peace so long as both men continued to breathe.

We know that both Perkin and Edward shared their beds with guards who were there for the purpose of not leaving either man alone. These guards were also conveyers of messages from the outside so that at all times Perkin and Edward were aware of the plans to save them. Whether the guards were motivated by Yorkist loyalty or Yorkist money, or both, depends on who recounts their stories. It is known too that the guards provided a human, comforting presence, as they were the same age as Perkins, 24, and Edward, also 24. Words and gestures of love between them were witnessed by others, sighs of lovemaking overhead, comforting solace, and the hope that at the end neither Perkin nor Edward lacked for living presence and understanding.

The four guardians responsible for Perkin and the four responsible for Edward were accused of treason for conspiring to free the prisoners. They were hanged until nearly dead, disemboweled, quartered (literally cut into four pieces) and beheaded. Edward was found guilty of treason and, thanks to his nobility, only beheaded. After all, he had been the son of a brother to two kings. Perkin was found guilty and hanged with the aid of a ladder that was carefully withdrawn, allowing the noose to tighten and gradually bring death by strangulation, as long as an hour later.

This unique son of man ended his short journey on an earth wondrously bountiful, heartbreakingly beautiful and totally uncaring, having known vicissitudes well beyond those of mere mortals, having given of himself, having known the true devotion of a good woman and that of a loyal friend, a loyal friend destined to die in the Battle of Flodden in 1513 at age 40.

CHAPTER THIRTEEN

BANQUET OF THE CHESTNUTS
The Borgia, Johann Burchard

Parties were thrown in Rome prior to her leaving the city, one of which, in 1501, was the famous Banquet of the Chestnuts, during which prizes were given to those who could ejaculate the most times and copulate with the most prostitutes. Some say Lucrezia was present. Some put Cesare there. Others place them both. All named Alexander.

Johann Burchard, a major chronicler during the Italian Renaissance, was the Borgia Master of Ceremonies, responsible for the preparation of festivities. He wrote in his diary *Liber Notarum*, in Latin, that the orgy took place in Cesare's Palazzo Apostolico on the 30th of October 1501: "Fifty honest prostitutes, called courtesans, danced after dinner with the attendants and others who were present, at first in their garments, then naked. After dinner the candelabra with the burning candles were taken from the tables and placed on the floor, and chestnuts were strewn around, which the naked courtesans picked up, creeping on hands and knees between the chandeliers, while the Pope, Cesare, and his sister **Lucrezia** looked on. Finally, prizes were announced for those who could perform the act most often with the courtesans, such as tunics of silk, shoes and other things." William Manchester in his *A World Lit Only by Fire*, wrote: "Servants kept score of each man's orgasms, for the pope greatly admired virility and measured a man's machismo by his ejaculatory capacity. After everyone was exhausted, His Holiness distributed prizes."

Many historians today reject outright that the orgy ever existed, which is nonetheless hard to do given Burchard's reputation for probity. Others insist that it not only existed, but had for purpose Alexander's intention of implicating the greatest number of cardinals possible, and then blackmailing them in order to get them to vote favorably on any measure for which Alexander needed their consent.

One observer stated that the orgy ended at noon on the 1st of November 1501 and had been a reversion to the paganism of the past.

CHAPTER FOURTEEN

LEONARDO DA VINCI
Salaì, Giovanni Melzi, Orazio Melzi, Giorgio Vasari, *The Vitruvian* Man, Giacomo Andrea, Cosimo de' Medici, François I

Leonardo da Vinci met Cesare when da Vinci was 50, Cesare 25, whom Leonardo found to be "the most handsome man in Italy." When Cesare and his army approached too closely to Florence for comfort, the city-state sent out Machiavelli and da Vinci as emissaries to appease him. Machiavelli became Cesare's riding companion and chief advisor, da Vinci Cesare's expert in the design of fortifications and other military engineering. It is thought that Leonardo's rides alongside Cesare through the Apennine Mountains provided the backdrop for his *Mona Lisa*.

Leonardo was gorgeous and so were his boys, beginning with Salaì, magnificent in da Vinci's two paintings, *St. John the Baptist* and *Bacchus*, the absolute ultimate in homoerotic art.

Da Vinci's *Bacchus*.

Salaì was Leonardo's nickname for his boy lover, meaning Little Devil, bestowed when Salaì, unmanageable and stubborn, hotheaded and careless, proved to be a liar and a not-so-accomplished--although highly assiduous--thief. This at the prepubescent age of ten. A very close friend of Leonardo's, Giacomo Andrea, was present during one of the first meals shared with Salaì. It is suspected that Leonardo's idea for the *Vitruvian Man,* the male body made up of two superimposed figures showing four arms and four legs, was originally Andrea's invention, and bares an amazing resemblance to Leonardo himself. Of Salaì Andrea said he was a glutton who ate as much as four monks, spilled the wine and broke whatever his fingers came upon. Another friend, the painter, architect, writer and historian Giorgio Vasari wrote that Salaì was "a graceful and beautiful boy with curly hair and a delight to Leonardo." There is no doubt that he was Leonardo's bedmate, the only question being from what age?

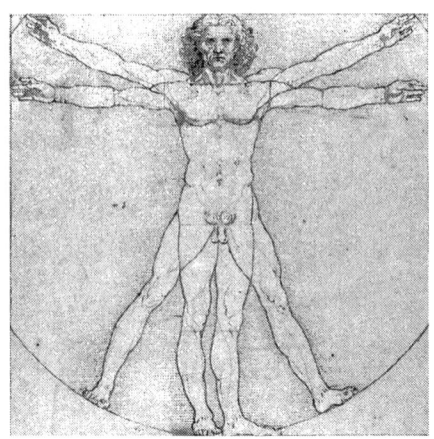

The Vitruvian Man

Numerous times Salaì made off with Leonardo's money, but as the painter had endless commissions, he was rich and, at the end of his life, even wealthy. Salaì is said to have bought clothes with most of the lucre he swiped, at one point possessing thirty pairs of shoes. Throughout his entire life he remained by Leonardo's side, at times replaced, as with the handsome Melzi, Melzi to whom Leonardo left half of his fortune, the other half going to Salaì. But most importantly, both boys remained loyal to the master, both present at his side to witness his last breath.

Some find it incomprehensible that Leonardo, known for his exactitude (most sources say it took him 4 years to paint the *Mona Lisa*, others as long as 14), painted *John the Baptist* as an erotic young man and not the usual old prophet in most paintings. The surprise is greater still when we learn that in Leonardo's painting the Baptist was at first totally nude, and that only later were animal skins added. At any rate, Leonardo kept the painting with him to the very end, understandable as *John the Baptist* is the most beautiful portrait of a young man that has ever been put on canvas. He kept the *Mona Lisa* until the very end too, at the Chateau of Clos Lucé, a chateau given to him by François I, who is believed to have held his head as he expired, perhaps his last gaze on Salaì at his bedside or Salaì, much younger, the model for *John the Baptist*.

John the Baptist

No one will ever know why the child Salaì was chosen by Leonardo. Leonardo himself said he had come upon him while the child was drawing, and seeing potential, he made enquiries into his family. Finding them poor, he made them an offer they couldn't refuse. Leonardo was thirty-eight, an age when a man begins to think of settling down, tired of running after boys his ever-so-slightly decline in beauty was more and more compensated for by a few easy coins, of which, for him, there was no dearth. Already, at age twenty-four, he'd been arrested by the Florentine Office of the Night, he and a gang of his friends, all accused of sodomy. He got off as the charge was difficult to prove, but it shows that, like other Florentines, he was no parvenu to male-male intercourse. His interest for those of his own sex was already well known, as reflected by the male nudes that studded his canvases and notebooks, erotic proof of the mystical attraction men have for each other. The boy Leonardo and his friends were accused of sodomizing was an apprentice goldsmith, Jacopo Salterelli, age 17, a notorious rent-boy. At that time in Florence there existed special letterboxes that citizens used to denounce other citizens, cited in the chapter on Botticelli. It was in this way that Leonardo and his companions had come to the attention of the authorities. There were two enquiries, at a month's distance, neither of which turned up enough evidence for a conviction, a conviction that held the death penalty, although if convicted one usually got off with a fine and a slap on the wrist, so common was the event. Serge Bramly in his *Leonardo* concludes: "The authorities were prepared to turn a blind eye to various sexual misdemeanors--homosexuality, incest, bigamy: fairly common forms of behavior, after all--on the condition that public order was not disturbed and that a minimum of discretion was observed." But Leonardo must have suffered nonetheless now that everyone in Florence knew about his indiscretion, including his father.

Leonardo's exposure to boys was literally limitless. In the workshop artists and their models came and went as they discussed artistic issues and gossiped, most of whom were sexually available. And as Leonardo gained in reputation, he was surrounded by a constantly renewed court of extremely beautiful boys and young men, friends and models, many of which adorned his paintings and notebooks: thighs, buttocks and penises from repose to full erection, or, in his words, "long, thick and heavy" to "short, slim and soft," and he continues: The male member "has a mind of its own. When we desire to stimulate it, it obstinately refuses, or the opposite. When a man is asleep it is awake, and when he's awake it's asleep. It remains inactive when we want action, and wants action when we forbid it." He maintains that "it" can at times be dangerous, inundating the world with human beings the world in no way needs, as well as being the entry point for diseases (syphilis having reached Italy in 1495).

The great art historian Giorgio Vasari wrote that "there is something supernatural in the accumulation in one person of so much beauty, grace, strength and intelligence as in da Vinci." Da Vinci was also said to be preternaturally gentle for the period, kind to rich and poor alike, generous, always in good humor and possessing a sense of humor. Vasari goes on to say, "Leonardo had such a great presence that one only had to see him for all sadness to vanish." As a person he personified what Plato would call the perfect alloy of *virtu*, intelligence and knowledge.

Leonardo was born, out-of-wedlock, in 1473 in the Tuscan hill town of Vinci, near the Arno River that flows through Florence.

His father was a wealthy legal notary and his mother a peasant. His full name was Leonardo di ser Piero da Vinci, meaning Leonardo son of Messer Piero from Vinci. He lived his first five years with his mother, then with his father who married four times, but never Leonardo's mother. He was a bastard but that had few ill effects in Renaissance Florence, although bastards couldn't be notaries, the position of his father which would certainly have become his own had he been born in wedlock--to the loss of the entire world had his destiny been such. He couldn't become a doctor, either, a pursuit he might well have chosen, given his love of science. In the case of bastards only the father's name was registered.

At age fourteen he was apprenticed to the painter Andrea di Cione, known to the world as Verrocchio, in whose *Archangel Michel* we see the incredibly beautiful Leonardo. The choice of Verrocchio was fortuitous as his paintings are exquisite, the demonstration that Fortune never ever stopped looking over Leonardo's shoulder. Verrocchio's shop was in Florence, another lucky break as it was then, as today, arguably the most beautiful city in the world. Verrocchio never married, but this was true of half of the male population of Florence for whom freedom to live their lives as they wished was of prime importance. Verrocchio's apprentices included Ghirlandaio, Botticelli and Botticini, whose *Tobias and the Three Archangels* features da Vinci. At age twenty Leonardo's father set him up with his own workshop, but his love for Verrocchio was such that they worked together until Verrocchio's death. Verrocchio was a father figure, perhaps the most important man in the artist's life.

Botticini's *Tobias and the Three Archangels,* da Vinci the angel on the left.

Verrocchio was described by Serge Bramly in his marvelous *Leonardo* as "a sort of one-man university of the arts." He knew and taught literally everything with the exception of huge wall murals, the reason for the disastrous destruction of the *Last Supper*. When Verrocchio was only 17 he had struck a boy, age 14, with a stone, killing him. He was jailed but released when it was proven that the incident had been an accident. Verrocchio was nonetheless haunted by what he had done to the very end, especially as he was a good man, sensitive in the extreme. Verrocchio's father died the year of the accident and Verrocchio found himself at the head of a family consisting of his mother and six brothers and sisters. Years later, now well-off, he was still providing for them as well as his nephews and nieces. Verrocchio was apprenticed to a goldsmith and began learning the skills of drawing, engraving, carving and metallurgy, followed by other jobs in which he would master sculpturing, painting, the basics of architecture and his favorite subject, mathematics. He was commissioned to make the tombstone for the person who started the Italian Renaissance, Cosimo de' Medici. Verrocchio established his own workshop, a large room with all the instruments an artist uses on the surrounding walls, plus sculptors' turntables, workbenches, easels and kiln, as well as shelves bent by the weight of busts and plaster body parts. Around the workshop and upstairs were the living quarters for the boys and the kitchen. An apprenticeship lasted around thirteen years, which started with sweeping the workshop and cleaning the materials, moved to the rudiments of drawing, making paintbrushes, preparing canvases and pigments freshly ground every day; sculpting, painting, drawing, decorating; even learning how to make salts out of human excrement--from dawn to dusk, seven days a week.

The workshop became the artistic center of Florence where one exchanged ideas, models, recipes for paint and varnishes, where philosophy was disputed and gossip swapped. Of special interest was the new Flemish technique for mixing paint with oil instead of water, making for brighter and more long-lasting colors and smoother gradations of tints, discussed in the life of Messina. Songs were sung and music was played, as Verrocchio was an accomplished musician. He was truly a kind of Pericles who created the conditions for geniuses to thrive--much of which was perhaps due to his attempt to compensate for having killed a lad of 14.

Like all boys, Leonardo liked to dress up and nowhere in world history was there a better, more exciting city than Florence under the Medici. The costumes for festivals and carnivals (designed by Verrocchio and company) were magnificent. Boys' trousers so tight they looked painted on, ample shirts that fell from the collar bones to the upper thighs, taken in by a thin belt at the waist, shirts that scarcely covered the piece of cloth over the genitals, held in place by two ribbons. A headband with perhaps a feather adorned the forehead. As Niccolò Machiavelli said, "The city's youth, being independent, spent excessive sums on clothing, feasting and debauchery. Living in idleness, it consumed its time and money on gaming and women."

At age twenty-four, as mentioned, Leonardo was arrested for sodomy. Four years later he moved in with the Medici, with Lorenzo *Il Magnifico*, thanks to whom commissions began to rain down on the lad. From there he went on to the career for which he is known the world over. Salaì followed in his footsteps, helping with his paintings, constructing the machines inspired by the master, keeping shop for the man who would reward him with a golden retirement, providing Salaì with a piece of land and the money on which to build a home. Salaì would later die in a duel, some say by sword, others by firearms, still others by a crossbow.

Salaì was the gift of God that those of my sexual persuasion could rightly give thanks for each and every day left to us on earth. A saner man than Leonardo would have thrown him out when the boy stole his first lire, or when caught in bed with another of the master's apprentices. But the genius whom we are all acquainted with, the master of every domain that took his interest, revered the boy as his source of inspiration, as the cherished love of his life. Leonardo could see beyond the daily tribulations and petty treasons. Instead, he held firm to the companion with whom he would walk the rocky path of life, right up to the end. That Salaì was beautiful and beautifully built was important, without doubt, but in a land like Italy, with apprentices he had to turn away in droves, he could have found a dozen replacements. Yet Leonardo knew that in the end one goes ahead alone or one grants the concessions necessary to share the route with another.

One of the most impressive realities concerning Leonardo's notebooks is that amidst the thousands of pages there is nearly nothing of a personal nature about the master himself. We have his thoughts, observations, calculations, recipes for mixing oils and ground paint, machines of all nature, fortification, anatomical drawings, male genitalia galore, the texts in reverse left-hand writing, much of which is illegible.

The second love of Leonardo's life was Giovanni Francesco Melzi who became his apprentice around 1508. The boy's father was a senator and a captain in Louis XII's army. Unlike Salaì who only partially succeeded as a painter, Giovanni Francesco Melzi did some remarkable works. As handsome as Leonardo had been in his youth, Giovanni followed his master to the end, inheriting half of his oeuvre. The Melzi family property was at Vaprio d'Adda, an enormous mansion, nearly a small Versailles, witness to the Melzi wealth. It was he who informed Leonardo's family of his master's death. Then he returned to Vaprio d'Adda with his master's notebooks and several paintings. He wrote a book drawn from Leonardo's observations about painting, which eventually found its way into the Vatican. The historian Vasari contacted Giovanni for help with the book he himself was writing. About Melzi Vasari wrote, "Sir Francesco Melzi, a Milanese gentleman, entered da Vinci's service as a young and extremely good-looking adolescent. He was very dear to his master and today is a noble and handsome old man." Giovanni left a son, Orazio, who sold off the notebooks bit by bit. His self-portrait, proof of Giovanni Melzi's wondrous beauty, can be found near my own home, at the Musée Bonnat, Bayonne France.

Giovanni Francesco Melzi/self-portrait.

Leonardo went to Milan where he was happy to put himself under the patronage of Ludovico Sforza who paid him extremely well and allowed him all the time he wanted in order to do exactly what Leonardo himself wished to do, and this for 18 years. Then Louis XII invaded Italy and Ludovico lost it all, eventually imprisoned by the French king until his death. Leonardo returned to Florence, age 48. The Medici had been expulsed and the Republic reestablished. Savonarola had gone up in smoke and a new breed of artist had arisen, led by Michelangelo and later by Raphael. His father was still there, age 74, with his forth wife and eleven children still at home, aged 2 to 24. Leonardo had written him often, always beginning with "Dearly beloved father..." a tender loving son, even if the reality of their closeness was perhaps other. At age 50 he hooked up with Cesare Borgia who appointed him military engineer, a position Bramly says he deeply desired.

Cesare was a bastard as was Leonardo, and Bramly goes on to say: "these two bastard children, having created their own lives, respected each other for their intelligence, independence of mind, and scorn for convention. Leonardo must also surely have been susceptible to Cesare's boisterous elegance and superb bearing." All certainly true as Cesare was virility personified. But unlike Leonardo, Cesare, age 27, was the adored son of his father, Pope Alexander VI, who would continue to love him even after Cesare murdered his brother, Juan--the son Alexander cherished even above Cesare. To have the backing and limitless wealth of his father, the pope, was a huge morale booster. Cesare went on a conquering spree and Machiavelli accompanied him. About Machiavelli's *Prince* Jean Giono wrote: "It is the most objective study of mankind to date, the study of passions treated dispassionately, as if solving a mathematical problem."

Both Michelangelo and da Vinci had only their love of men in common. The painted nudes of Michelangelo were peaches-and-cream clean, those of da Vinci homoerotic wet dreams (although Michelangelo's statues were, homoerotically speaking, to die for). The first, da Vinci, had been handsome, the second, Michelangelo, never. The first was now old, the second just starting out on the road to eternal glory. Vasari tells us that it was around this time that a boy, 20, living in Urbino, decided to forget everything he had ever learned about art and dedicate himself to copying Leonardo's paintings, paintings that had just come to his attention. The boy had a magnificent name, Raphael.

Leonardo went to Milan where the French reserved a wonderful reception for him, as Louis XII was the reincarnation of the Renaissance itself. He started the *Mona Lisa* but the history of the painting is far to complicated to be approached here. It's the Churchillian riddle wrapped in a mystery inside an enigma. We're not sure even who ordered it, let alone who sat for it, although many think it was Salaì himself. (Michelangelo always had men pose for his statues of woman, as well as some portraits.)

While battles for and against Louis XII whirled around him, Leonardo was creating another work whose importance would span a period of 500 years: it was a study of the human body, dissected with perfection and drawn with a detail that takes one's breath away. In his own words (and 200 illustrations) he tells of accompanying an old man in his last hours, how the man complained of no physical pain, only weakness, and how he gently slipped from life into death. To find out the cause Leonardo did an autopsy, discovering that the artery supply to the heart and lower members had withered, describing, for the first time in the history of medicine, arteriosclerosis. Bramly takes over: "One wonders what it felt like to plunge a knife into the thorax of an old man one had been speaking to not long before." Later in his notes Leonardo describes examining a hanged man, his penis engorged, of which he made detailed drawings. Leonardo went on to say that even if one had a love for dissecting, one's stomach might find it disgusting, and one might "be afraid to stay up at night in the company of corpses cut to pieces and lacerated and horrible to behold."

Politically, there was movement. Ludovico Sforza's son Massimiliano Sforza recovered Milan, expulsing the French back across the Alps. Pope Julius II died and was replaced by Leo X, the youngest son of Lorenzo *Il Magnifico,* enabling the Medici to reconquer Florence after twenty years of disgrace, and bring an end to the Republic. Leo X was destined to die of gout, as did the majority of the Medici, so rich they could afford the richest food (the cause of gout), but Leo X surpassed them all in girth. He had nonetheless brought a cultural revolution to Rome and was flattered by his followers as he who introduced the reign of Apollo, an esthetic age of gold. Leo X's brother, Giuliano de' Medici, one of many patrons of art supposed to have commissioned the *Mona Lisa,* convinced Leonardo to come to the Eternal City where the artist found himself eclipsed by the new stars of the Renaissance, Michelangelo, Titian and Raphael, Raphael who was paid 12,000 ducats for his works, while da Vinci was offered a measly 33 ducats a month, bringing the quip to Leonardo's mouth, "The Medici created me and destroyed me." He was now old, but his greatest triumphs, his *St. John the Baptist* and his *Mona Lisa* were still to come. He spent three unhappy years in the service of Giuliano, part of which was dedicated to building canals that would drain fever-breeding swamps from around Rome--aided by the intelligent Melzi. The works he initiated were completed 300 years later.

Finally came his encounter with the man with whom he would end his life, François I, age 19, a giant at more than 6 feet, who loved war, placing himself in the front lines, and was an insatiable womanizer. He recaptured Milan and Ludovico's son Massimiliano Sforza, but instead of throwing him into a dungeon he welcomed the lad to his court and pensioned him off. Leonardo went to the Loire Valley, but only after the death of Giuliano de' Medici. The year was 1516; da Vinci had 3 years left to him. He became François's tutor, and their days and nights were filled with discussion, often in the presence of Salaì and Melzi, all three immeasurable comforts to the old man, old beyond his years as we see in his self-portrait. Personally, I have never, ever come across a life as perfect as de Vinci's; never has there been a man as deserving of the name Man.

The last words will be Melzi's, in a letter he sent to Leonardo's surviving brothers: "He was the best of fathers to me and the grief I feel at his death is impossible to express. As long as I have breath I shall feel an eternal sadness, for every day he gave me proof of a passionate and ardent affection. Each of us will mourn the loss of a man such that nature is powerless to create another."

POSTSCRIPT

As the reader now knows, nothing in this book was written to titillate the imagination. Scores of books and films have been made on the Borgia, none, as far as I'm concerned, worthy of Michael Hirst's televised series on another family, *The Tudors*. Mario Puzo of *Godfather* fame had a lifelong interest in the Borgia, and one scene from his book, *The Family*, has Alexander VI writing at his table, while in a corner Cesare is attempting to penetrate his sister Lucrezia. Complaining that he's hurting her, Alexander goes to the bed and instructs the boy on how to make her passionate enough to want his entry. Another scene in Puzo's book has Cesare in a *hot tub* with Astorre Manfredi, although in this case it concerns a natural rock cavity fed by warm spring water. The television Showtime *The Borgias* is as historically ridiculous as Puzo's inventions, although it did gain an award for outstanding costumes, which, along with exterior and interior décors are, to say the least, sumptuous.

Every part of the drama that took place 500 years ago is disputed, and nothing is expected to turn up in some monastery that will enlighten us further, the reason why I've based this work on those actually present, Burchard and Machiavelli, the first who may have had, or not had, an axe to grind against his employers, the Borgia, the second who truly loved and admired the man he rode beside, Cesare Borgia, thanks to whom Machiavelli is known worldwide for his *The Prince*.

SOURCES

(1) See my book *British Homosexuality*.
(2) See my book *Hadrian and Antinous*.
(3) See my book *TROY*.
(4) See my book *Florence*.
(5) See my book *Cellini*.
(6) See my book *Omnisexuality*.
(7) See my book *Henry III*.
(8) See my book *Five Renaissance Wonders*.

Ady, Cecilia, *A History of Milan under the Sforza*, 1907.
Baglione, *Caravaggio*, circa 1600.
Barber, Richard, *The Devil's Crown--Henry II and Sons*, 1978.
Bellori, *Caravaggio*, circa 1600.
Bergreen, Laurence, *Over the Edge of the World. Magellan.* 2003.
Bicheno, Hugh, *Vendetta*, 2007.
Blanchard, Jean-Vincent, *Éminence, Cardinal Richelieu and the Rise of*
Boyd, Douglas, *April Queen*, 2004.
Boyles, David, *Blondel's Song*, 2005.
Bramly, Serge, *Leonardo*, 1988. A wonderful book.
Calimach, Andrew, *Lover's Legends*, 2002.
Carroll, Stuart, *Maryrs & Murderers, The Guise Family*, 2009.
Cawthorne, Nigel, *Sex Lives of the Popes*, 1996
Cellini, Benvenuto, *The Autobiography of Benvenuto Cellini*.
Chamberlin, E.R. *The Fall of the House of Borgia*, 1974

Cloulas, Ivan, *The Borgia*, 1989.
Cooper, John, *The Queen's Agent*, 2011.
Crompton, Louis, *Homosexuality and Civilization*, 2003.
Crowley, Roger, *Empires of the Sea*, 2008. Marvelous.
Dale, Richard, *Who Killed Sir Walter Raleigh?* 2011.
Davidson, James, *Courtesans and Fishcakes*, 1998.
Davis, John Paul, *The Gothic King, Henry III*, 2013.
Erlanger, Philippe, *The King's Minion*, 1901.
Forellino, Antonio, *Michelangelo*, 2005. Beautiful reproductions.
Frieda, Leonie, *Catherine de Medici*, 2003.
Gayford, Martin, *Michelangelo*, 2013. A beautiful book.
Gillingham, John, *Richard the Lionheart*, 1978.
Graham-Dixon, Andrew, *Caravaggio* 2010. Fabulous.
Grazia, Sebastian de, *Machiavelli in Hell*, 1989.
Guicciardini, *Storie fiorentine (History of Florence)*, 1509.
Halperin David M. *One Hundred Years of Homosexuality*, 1990.
Hibbert, Christopher, *Florence, the Biography of a City*, 1993.
Hibbert, Christopher, *The Borgias and Their Enemies*, 2009.
Hibbert, Christopher, *The Rise and Fall of the House of Medici*, 1974.
Hicks, Michael, *Richard III*, 2000.
Hine, Daryl, *Puerilities*, 2001.
Hughes-Hallett, *Heroes*, 2004.
Hutchinson, Robert, *Elizabeth's Spy Master*, 2006.
Hutchinson, Robert, *House of Treason*, 2009.
Hutchinson, Robert, *Thomas Cromwell*, 2007.
Jack, Belinda, *Beatrice's Spell*, 2004.
Johnson, Marion, *The Borgias*, 1981.
Lacey, Robert, *Henry VIII*, 1972.
Lambert, Gilles *Caravaggio*, 2007.
Landucci, Luca, *A Florentine Diary*, around 1500, a vital source.
Lev, Elizabeth, *The Tigress of Forli*, 2011. Wonderfully written.
Levy, Buddy, *Conquistador*, 2009.
Levy, Buddy, *River of Darkness*, 2011. Fabulous.
Lubkin, Gregory, *A Renaissance Court*, 1994.
Lyons, Mathew, *The Favourite*, 2011.
Mackay, James, *In My End is My Beginning, Mary Queen of Scots*, 1999.
Mallett, Michael and Christine Shaw, *The Italian Wars 1494-1559*.
Manchester, William, *A World Lit Only By Fire*, 1993.
Mancini, *Caravaggio*, circa 1600.
Martines, Lauro, *April Blood-Florence and the Plot against the Medici*, 2003.
McLynn, Frank, *Richard and John, Kings of War*, 2007. Fabulous.
Meyer, G.J. *The Borgias, The Hidden History*, 2013.
Miller, David, *Richard the Lionheart*, 2003.

Moote, Lloyd, *Louis XIII, The Just*, 1989.
Mortimer, Ian, 1415, *Henry V's Year of Glory*, 2009.
Nicholl, Charles, *The Reckoning*, 2002.
Noel, Gerard, *The Renaissance Popes*, 2006.
Parker, Derek, *Cellini*, 2003, the book is beautifully written.
Pascal, Jean Claude, *L'Amant du Roi*, 1991.
Payne, Robert and Nihita Romanoff, *Ivan the Terrible*, 2002.
Pernot, Michel, *Henri III*, Le Roi Décrié, 2013, Excellent book.
Petitfils, Jean-Christian, *Louis XIII*, 2008, wonderful.
Pollard, .J., *Warwick the Kingmaker*, 2007.
Read, Piers Paul, *The Templars*, 1999.
Reston, James, *Warriors of God, Richard and the Crusades*, 2001.
Ridley, Jasper, *The Tudor Age*, 1998.
Robb, Peter, M – *The Man Who Became Caravaggio*, 1998.
Robb, Peter, *Street Fight in Naples*, 2010.
Rocke, Michael, *Forbidden Friendships*, 1996. Fabulous/indispensible.
Ross, Charles, *Richard III*, 1981.
Ruggiero, Guido, *The Boundaries of Eros*, 1985.
Sabatini, Rafael, *The Life of Cesare Borgia*, 1920.
Saslow, James, *Ganymede in the Renaissance*, 1986.
Saslow, James, *Ganymede in the Renaissance*, 1986.
Seward, Desmond, *Caravaggio – A Passionate Life*, 1998.
Simonetta, Marcello, *The Montefeltro Conspiracy*, 2008. Wonderful.
Skidmore, Chris, *Death and the Virgin*, 2010.
Skidmore, *Death and the Virgin*, 2007.
Solnon, Jean-Fançois, *Henry III*, 1996.
Strathern, Paul, *The Medici, Godfathers of the Renaissance*, 2003. Superb.
Stuart, Stirling, *Pizarro - Conqueror of the Inca*, 2005.
Unger Miles, *Magnifico, The Brilliant Life and Violent Times*
Unger, Miles, *Machiavelli*, 2008.
Vasari, We would know next to nothing if it were not for him.
Vernant, Jean-Pierre, *Mortals and Immortals*, 1991.
Viroli, Maurizio, *Niccolo's Smile, A Biography of Machiavelli*, 1998.
Warren, W.L., *Henry II*, 1973.
Weir, Alison, *Eleanor of Aquitaine*, 1999. Weir is a fabulous writer.
Weir, Alison, *Mary, Queen of Scots*, 2003.
Weir, Alison, *The Princes in the Tower*, 1992. Marvelous.
Weir, Alison, *The Wars of the Roses*, 1995.
Wikipedia: Research today is impossible without the aid of this monument.
Wilson, Derek, *The Uncrowned Kings of England*, 2005.
Wright, Ed, *History's Greatest Scandals*, 2006.
Wroe, Ann, *Perkin, A Story of Deception*, 2003. Fabulous

INDEX

Please note that the page numbers are *passim*. An example, Juan Borgia 76 – 102 means that Juan Borgia is found within these pages, but not necessarily on *every* page.

Agnadello, Battle of 108-119
Albert, Amanieu d' 66-74
Alègre, Yves d' Corella, Micheletto de 102-108
Alexander VI *passim*
Alfonso II 51-60
Alfonso of Naples and Aragon 60-66, 66-74
Alfonso V 38-51
Amboise, George d' 66-74, 119-126
Andrea, Giacomo 142-153
Aubigny, Bernard Stewart d' 92-102
Bande Nere, Giovanni dalle 92-102
Banquet of the Chestnuts 10-16, 74-92
Baptistery of San Giovanni 16-32
Barbarossa 10-16, 108-119
Barbo, Pietro 38-51
Barcelona, Treaty of 108-119
Baroncelli, Bernardo 32-38
Bembo, Pietro 119-126
Bembo, Pietro 74-92
Bentivoglio, Ermes 102-108
Bentivoglio, Francesca 74-92, 92-102
Bentivoglio, Giovanni 92-102, 102-108
Borgia, Alonso 38-51
Borgia, Cesare *passim*
Borgia, Jofrè 51-60, 60-66, 119-126
Borgia, Juan 38-51, 60-66
Borgia, Lucrezia *passim*
Borgia, Pierluigi 38-51
Botticelli 16-32
Brunelleschi, Filippo 16-32
Burchard, Johann 10-16, 92-102, 119-126, 141
Calderon, Pedro 60-66
Calixtus III 38-51
Cambrai, League of 108-119
Caravaggio 10-16
Carlotta of Navarre 66-74
Casanova, Cardinal 119-126

158

Catanei, Vannozza de' 38-51
Cateau-Cambrésis, Treaty of 108-119
Caterina Riario Sforza 10-16
Cathedral of Santa Maria del Fiore 16-32
Catherine of Aragon 60-66
Cellini 10-16
Charles V 108-119
Charles VII 16-32
Charles VIII 51-60, 126-141
Chestnuts, Banquet of the 10-16
Cione, Andrea di 142-153
Clarence, brother of Edward IV 126-141
Clement VII 108-119
Clement VIII 38-51
Clockwork Orange 10-16
Cognac, League of 108-119
Colleoni, Bartolommeo 16-32
Colloredo, Asquino de 102-108
Corella, Micheletto de (see Micheletto)
Crépy, Peace of 108-119
Donatello 16-32
Down and Dirty, The 38-51
Dracula 16-32
Edward IV 126-141
Edward VI 108-119
Elizabeth I 108-119
Erasmus 74-92
Este, Alfonso d' 7-92, 119-126
Este, Ercole d' 74-92
Este, Ferrante, d' 119-126
Este, Giulio d' 119-126
Este, Ippolito d' 119-126
Estouteville, Cardinal d' 38-51
Eugene IV 38-51
Faenza 92-102
Fano, Bishop of 66-74
Farnese Pier Luigi 108-119
Farnese, Alessandro 38-51
Farnese, Giulia 38-51
Farnese, Ottavio 108-119
Feo, Bernardino 74-92
Feo, Giacomo 74-92
Ferdinand of Spain 108-119

Ferdinand, King of Spain 108-119, 126-141
Ferrante I, King of Naples 16-32, 32-38, 38-51, 51-60
Ferrari, Gianbattista 119-126
François I 108-119, 142-153
Frederick IV 51-60
Frederick of Naples 60-66
Ghiberti, Lorenzo 16-32
Giovanni dalle Bande Nere 92-102
Giustinian, Ambassador 119-126
Gonzaga, Francesco 119-126
Gonzaga, Rodolfo 66-74
Great Schism 38-51
Gutenberg Press 74-92
Hadrian, Emperor 74-92
Henry II 108-119
Henry VII 126-141
Henry VII 51-60, 92-102
Henry VIII 60-66, 108-119, 119-126
Innocent VIII 38-51, 74-92
Isabella, Queen of Spain 119-126, 126-141
James IV 126-141
Julius II *passim*
Knights of St. John 10-16
Lampugnano 32-38
Landriani, Lucrezia 74-92
Last Judgment 38-51
Leo X 92-102, 108-119
Lippi, Filippino 16-32
Lippi, Filippo 16-32
Lorca, Ramiro da 102-108
Lorca, Ramiro de Corella, Micheletto de 102-108
Lorenzino 108-119
Louis XII 51-66, 74-102, 108-119
Luther, Martin 108-119
Machiavelli, Niccolò 10-16, 66-74, 92-102,142-153
Madrid, Treaty of 108-119
Malatesta, Carlo II 66-74
Malatesta, Ferrantino 66-74
Malatesta, Giovanni 66-74
Malatesta, Novello 66-74
Malatesta, Pandolfo I 66-74
Malatesta, Paolo 66-74
Malatesta, Ramberto 66-74

Malatesta, Roberto 66-74
Malatesta, Sallustio 66-74
Malatesta, Sigismondo Pandolfo 66-74
Malatesta, Valerio 66-74
Manfredi, Astorre 74-92, 74-92, 92-102
Manfredi, Galeotto 74-92
Manfredi, Gianevangelista 92-102
Manfredi, Ottaviano 74-92
Margaret of Burgundy 126-141
Martin V 38-51
Maximilian I, Holy Roman Emperor 108-119, 126-141
Medici, Alessandro de 108-119
Medici, Caterina Riario Sforza de' (see Sforza, Caterina)
Medici, Cosimo de' 16-32, 142-153
Medici, Giovanni de' 74-92, 92-102, 108-119
Medici, Giovanni Sforza de' 74-92
Medici, Giuliano de' 32-38
Medici, Lorenzo de' 16-32, 32-38, 74-92
Medici, Marie de' 92-102
Medici, Piero de' 16-32, 51-60
Melzi, Giovanni Francesco 142-153
Melzi, Orazio 142-153
Michelangelo 38-51, 119-126
Micheletto 66-74, 102-108, 119-126
Michiel, Giovanni 119-126
Mila, Adriana da 38-51
Montefeltro 32-38
Montefeltro, Federico da 16-32, 32-38
Montefeltro, Guidobaldo da 119-126
Montefletro, Federico da 16-32
More, Thomas 74-92
Navarre, Juan of 119-126 119-126
Nicholas III 74-92
Nicholas V 16-32
Office of the Night 16-32, 142-153
Olgiati, Girolamo 32-38
Oliverotto of Fermo 102-108
Ordelaffi, Antonio Maria 74-92
Ordelaffi, Francesco 74-92
Ordelaffi, Pino 74-92
Orsini, Francesco 102-108
Orsini, Magione 102-108
Orsini, Paolo 102-108

Orsini, Roberto 102-108
Papal States 38-51
Parentucelli 16-32
Paul II 38-51
Paul III 38-51, 108-119
Pazzi, Francesco de' 32-38
Pazzi, Jacopo de' 32-38
Peo, Giacomo 74-92
Perkin 126-141
Petrucci, Pandolfo 102-108
Philip I 126-141
Philip II 108-119
Philippe II 126-141
Piccolomini, Cardinal 38-51
Pius II 16-32, 38-51, 66-74
Pius III 102-108, 119-126
Primavera 16-32
Queen Joanna of Naples 38-51
Ravaldino 74-92
Revolt of the Condottieri 102-108
Riario, Bianca 74-92
Riario, Girolamo 32-38, 74-92
Riario, Ottaviano 74-92
Riario, Raffaelle 38-51
Richard I 126-141
Richard III 126-141
Romagna, The 66-74
Rovere, Francesco della 119-126
Rovere, Giuliano della 38-51, 51-60, 119-126
Salaì 142-153
Salterelli, Jacopo 142-153
Salviati, Francesco 32-38
Salviati, Jacopo 92-102
San Giovanni, Baptistery of 16-32
Sancia 51-60
Santa Maria del Fiore 16-32
Savelli, Bishop 74-92
Savonarola 10-16, 32-38, 51-60
Scarampo, Cardinal 38-51
Scola, Ettore 38-51
Sforza, Caterina 10-16, 32-38, 38-51, 74-92, 92-102
Sforza, Francesco 16-32, 108-119
Sforza, Galeazzo Maria 16-32, 32-38, 38-51, 51-60, 74-102

Sforza, Gian Galeazzo 51-60
Sforza, Giovanni 51-60, 60-66
Sforza, Ludovico 51-60, 74-92, 142-153
Sforza, Massimiliano 108-119
Sforza, Polissena 66-74
Siena 92-102
Simnel 126-141
Sixtus IV 32-38, 38-51, 66-74, 74-92
Skanderbeg of Albania 38-51
Soderini, Francesco 92-102
Soderini, Francesco 92-102
Strappando 92-102
Swiss Guard 119-126
Syphilis 51-60, 66-74
Tale of Two Lovers 16-32
Torrigiano, Pietro 66-74
Vannozza 119-126
Vasari, Giorgio 142-153
Verrocchio 142-153
Vinci, Leoanrdo da 74-92, 142-153
Visconti, Carlo 32-38
Visconti, Filippo Maria 16-32
Visconti, Gian Maria 16-32
Visconti, Maria Filippo 38-51
Vitelli, Paolo 102-108
Vitelli, Vitellozzo 102-108
Vitruvian Man, The 142-153
Volterra, Danielle da 38-51
War of the Roses 126-141
Warbeck, Perkin 126-141

Printed in Great Britain
by Amazon